INTERNATIONAL COMMUNISM IN LATIN AMERICA:
A History of the Movement, 1917–1963

Studies in Contemporary Latin America
JOHN J. JOHNSON, STANFORD UNIVERSITY
GENERAL EDITOR

THE ARTS IN LATIN AMERICA
*By Gilbert Chase, Inter-American Institute for Musical
Research, Tulane University*

GOVERNMENT AND POLITICS IN
LATIN AMERICA
*By Philip J. Taylor, School of Advanced International
Studies, The Johns Hopkins University*

ORGANIZED LABOR IN LATIN AMERICA
By Robert J. Alexander, Rutgers University

NATIONALISM IN CONTEMPORARY
LATIN AMERICA
*By Arthur P. Whitaker, University of Pennsylvania, and
David Jordan, The Pennsylvania State University*

INTERNATIONAL COMMUNISM IN
LATIN AMERICA
By Rollie E. Poppino, University of California, Davis

INTERNATIONAL
COMMUNISM
IN
LATIN AMERICA

A HISTORY OF THE MOVEMENT 1917–1963

Rollie E. Poppino

University of California, Davis

THE FREE PRESS, *New York*

Collier-Macmillan Limited, *London*

Copyright © 1964 by The Free Press of Glencoe

A DIVISION OF THE MACMILLAN COMPANY

Printed in the United States of America

Collier-Macmillan Canada, Ltd., Toronto, Ontario

Library of Congress Catalog Card Number: 64–21203

Second Printing May 1966

Contents

Contents

Preface

THIS VOLUME BY PROFESSOR ROLLIE POPPINO IS THE FIRST IN
The Free Press series of original studies on Contemporary Latin
America. The Free Press, as publisher, and I, as general editor of
the series, are proud that it is being launched by such a timely
and searching study.

Professor Poppino, of the Department of History at the University of California, Davis, was for seven years (1954–61) with the
Department of State; for the last four of those years he has closely
followed Communist and Castroist activities and strategies in all
of Latin America, but especially in currently troubled Brazil. His
study reflects both the scholarly objectivity of the academic and
the concerns of the activist who must be prepared to make on-
the-spot decisions.

Poppino has written an important book and in some respects
a unique one; important in that he skillfully synthesizes earlier
exploratory studies while giving due attention to recent developments, unique in that he focuses on areas which have been
neglected in the past but an acquaintance with which is essential to
a fuller understanding of communism and Castroism in Latin
America. His treatment of Soviet relations with Latin American
Communist parties, for example, adds a new and valuable dimen-
sion to the historical evolution of communism in this hemisphere.
But Poppino is nowhere more at home or on surer ground
than when he relates communism to the rapid, often revolutionary, changes that have been taking place in the political,
social, and economic structures of the twenty republics. His
sections on the appeals of communism to people who are for-

vii

saking traditional institutions before they have evolved acceptable new ones are disconcertingly convincing.

Poppino does not provide pat formulas for combatting communism in Latin America; he knows the Communists too well to be deceived into believing that there is at a given moment only one way to treat with them. He does, however, offer an attractive list of alternative ways of dealing with the Communist "problem." In a world in which politicians, journalists, and, too often, scholars are quick to offer simple solutions to complex problems, Poppino's dispassionate discussion of possible approaches to containing communism and Castroism in Latin America serves to emphasize the sense of realism and reasonableness that the author displays throughout the study.

JOHN J. JOHNSON
Department of History
Stanford University
Stanford, California

I.

Why Communism in Latin America?

ONE

The Confident Communists

IT IS ONE OF THE APPARENT PARADOXES OF OUR TIME, AND A CAUSE for great concern in the United States, that international communism has been able to gain a strong foothold in the Western Hemisphere and is picking up momentum in its drive to capture the allegiance of the peoples of Latin America. After forty years of limited prospects and meager accomplishments, the Communist movement seems to be catching fire among the twenty republics to the south. Cuba, which for six decades was intimately associated with the United States, has suddenly and dramatically identified itself with the Soviet bloc in the cold war, has openly embraced Marxism-Leninism, and is calling upon the rest of Latin America to follow its lead. Everywhere the Communists have seized upon the Cuban issue and are making it their principal rallying cry. From Mexico in the north to Chile in the far south they display growing confidence in the inevitable victory of their cause. In at least half of the republics, where the Communist appeal to the oppressed and discontented is on the rise, the Communists reflect the conviction that, by votes or violence, the masses will soon sweep them into power as the guiding force in so-called governments of "national liberation."

Where law or political practice permits, the Communists run candidates for public office. They now campaign under their own banner whenever possible. When this cannot be done they seek accommodations with other parties and present their candidates under other labels. Avowed or disguised Communists occupy seats in the national, state, or municipal legislatures of at least seven Latin American republics in addition to Cuba, where the

Communist party controls the bulk of the offices normally filled by election. Ostensibly, by participating in electoral activities, the Communists are attempting to demonstrate their political respectability and their faith in Premier Khrushchev's assertion that the "transition to socialism" can be achieved by orderly, constitutional means. As a practical matter, Latin American Communists in public office exploit their positions by using them as forums from which to oppose the programs of present governments and to advocate Cuban-style reorganization of the society, the economy, and the political system. Invariably their proposals include the adoption of a pro-Soviet, anti-United States foreign policy.

In the past few years the chief characteristics of many of the Latin American Communist parties has been boldness in advocating violence as a political weapon. Despite their protestations that the road to communism need not be a violent one, Communists outside of Chile have shown increasing willingness to call openly for revolution and, at times, to risk a show of force, as Communists, against local authorities. Rioting, sometimes Communist-led and more often Communist-inspired, has become commonplace in several of the larger cities since the visit of former Vice-President Richard Nixon to Latin America in 1958. While Latin American host governments have since been able to prevent a recurrence of hostile demonstrations against visiting dignitaries from the United States, these governments themselves have frequently been the target of communist attacks and subversion. Since 1959 Communists have participated in, and have frequently claimed responsibility for, armed invasions and barracks revolts designed to overthrow the governments of nearly half of the countries of the area.

In most of the Latin American countries the Communists are extending their operations to the rural areas and are competing seriously with noncommunist leftist parties for a following among the land-hungry peasant masses. Like Communist parties everywhere, those in Latin America have long claimed to represent both peasants and urban workers, but in fact they are overwhelmingly urban in membership. In the past the Communists were usually unable, and frequently unwilling, to appeal effectively to the rural lower classes, who have traditionally been excluded from active participation in national politics. However, since the victory of the Cuban revolution, agrarian reform has become a burning issue in a majority of the republics, and the Communists are contributing to make all but the most remote peasant communities aware of it. They present themselves to the unsophisticated rural populace as the originators of agrarian reform and call for the wholesale confiscation and redistribution of large private landholdings. In several countries, where comparatively moderate agrarian reform programs have been enacted or proposed, they are using direct action or the threat of violence in an attempt to undermine noncommunist approaches to the problem and to force the adoption of land redistribution programs based on the Cuban model. Thus, Communist agitators have urged isolated peasant bands in El Salvador, Colombia, Ecuador, and Peru to seize the estates on which they work as virtual serfs. In Brazil, Francisco Julião, the radical leader of peasant leagues in the poverty-stricken Northeast and the self-conscious disciple of Fidel Castro, has threatened to lead his followers in a bloody revolution unless his demands for sweeping social and economic reforms are promptly met.

The optimism that pervades the Latin American Communist parties appears amply justified not only by the ability of the Communists to take advantage of mob violence in the larger cities, to lead or take part in the increasingly frequent armed attacks on certain governments, and to make inroads among the stirring rural masses, but also, perhaps most of all, by the capacity of the Socialist revolution in Cuba to survive in the face of opposition by the United States and three-quarters of the countries of Latin America. The apparent strength and prospects of the Communist movement have led many observers to question whether even the ten-year, $20-billion Alliance for Progress program, initiated during the administration of John F. Kennedy, can stem the tide and prevent much of Latin America from falling into the Communist camp. The Latin American Communists confidently and vociferously boast that it cannot. They maintain that Latin America must inevitably adopt Cuban-style "Socialist republics," or Communist-oriented governments of "national liberation." They insist that the existence of the powerful Soviet Union makes it impossible for the United States to impose its will by force, and that if the leaders of Latin America do not accept Communist counsel and cooperation they will be overthrown by revolution from below.

There is little room for complacency with regard to the potential threat posed by the Communist movement in Latin America. Yet, an examination of the present size, status, and political role of the various Communist parties indicates that in nearly every instance the Communists greatly exaggerate both their capabilities and immediate prospects.

The sharp rise in the level of Communist confidence and militancy does not reflect comparable increases in party membership and electoral following in most of Latin America. In fact, the Communist parties over-all now have a net increase of less than 10 per cent over the approximately 200,000 members they had in the early 1950's. Even if the several Trotskyist parties, the Communist-front Socialist People's Party of Vicente Lombardo Toledano in Mexico, and the entire membership of the Cuban United Party of the Socialist Revolution are included in the tabulation, the total still falls well below the combined Latin American Communist party memberships in the immediate postwar period and represents less than 0.2 per cent of the current population of the area. Despite the Communist parties operating generally in a highly favorable political climate in Latin America, their expansion has barely managed to keep pace with the rate of population growth in the past decade.

Observations about the over-all strength of the Communist parties on a per capita basis serve to obscure striking disparities in party membership and effectiveness among the twenty republics. The fortunes of the various Communist organizations have by no means been uniform in recent years. Some of them are larger or more effective than at any time in the past. Others, once significant, have never regained the influence and following they enjoyed in the era of good feeling between Communists and noncommunists during World War II. The largest group of Communist parties, including perhaps half the total, continues as it has always done to exist on the lunatic fringe of national politics, still expectantly waiting for the opportunity to play a significant role in the political arena.

*   *   *

Obviously, the Communist party in Cuba, the Popular Socialist Party, is currently the most successful Communist organization in the Western Hemisphere. From illegal status and clandestine, carefully circumscribed activities after 1953, under the Batista dictatorship, it emerged with Castro's victory as the only effective political organization on the island. The Communists are now at least co-partners with Castro in the formulation of the policies of his regime. Significantly, in their campaign to present themselves as loyal and subservient to Castro, Cuban Communist leaders did not take advantage of the abundant opportunities to rebuild the mass party they commanded in the 1940's, when Communist candidates polled 150,000 votes. Rather, they preferred to maintain a tightly knit following of tested and dedicated Communist militants. This following probably did not exceed 30,000 in 1961, when the Popular Socialist Party was incorporated into the government's Integrated Revolutionary Organizations. Moreover, although all organized supporters of the Castro regime now call themselves Marxist-Leninists, it is likely that not more than half the 80,000-odd members of the new United Party of the Socialist Revolution, inaugurated in February 1963, can be regarded as disciplined Communists. Nevertheless, "old" Communists hold key positions in the state political apparatus and exploit it as an extension of their own party.

*   *   *

The overthrow of dictatorships in Colombia in 1957 and Venezuela in 1958 permitted the Communist parties of these countries to regain legal status. In Colombia the government's policy of guaranteeing civil liberties to all citizens has enabled the Communists to expand their propaganda activities, but the exclusion of all minor parties from political office under the current National Front agreement between the traditional Conservative and Liberal parties has seriously hampered communist efforts to attract broad popular support. Under the circumstances the Colombian Communists have dissipated much of their energy in factionalism. The Communist Party of Colombia—split into at least four distinct groups, with as many rival leaders—remains one of the lesser protest parties in the country.

In Venezuela, where Communists played an active role in the overthrow of the Pérez Jiménez regime and helped to write the electoral code which restored legal recognition to the party, the Communist apparatus is one of the strongest on the mainland of Latin America. Party membership has more than tripled to at least thirty thousand, and the Communists have demonstrated their ability to elicit over five times that many votes from the electorate at large. Competing vigorously in the national elections of 1958, the party polled over 160,000 votes, better than 6 per cent of the total, to place two of its members in the Senate and seven in the National Congress. After failing to gain an influential voice in the Betancourt administration, the Communists led their following into the opposition and created a clandestine paramilitary apparatus that cooperates closely with noncommunist leftist extremists. The party is split into three factions, which appear to be divided chiefly over the tactics required to topple the government.

*   *   *

In the Dominican Republic prospects for the Communist movement improved for a time following the fall of the Trujillo dictatorship, but have again deteriorated. At best the Communists operated under serious handicaps. Since virtually all Dominican Communists were known to have escaped the hardships of the later years of the dictatorship in exile in neighboring republics, after Trujillo's assassination in May 1961 they were unable, as Communists, to make good their bid for leadership of those who had remained in the country. Moreover, the provisional post-Trujillo administrations effectively banned overt Communist political activity. Under the circumstances the Communists appeared to abandon their customary vehicle, the Popular Socialist Party, and its most prominent leaders, who made their headquarters in Cuba.

The balance of the Communist exiles returned to their homeland, presenting themselves as revolutionary nationalists. Working through a succession of political front organizations, they penetrated noncommunist leftist parties and competed vigorously with representatives of democratic forces for control of the emerging labor movement.

The left-of-center Bosch administration, which took office in February 1963, was overthrown by the armed forces the following September, in part for permitting known Communists to return to the Dominican Republic. While fear of communism appears not to have been the chief concern of the army generals, their seizure of power abruptly canceled the limited Communist gains. Over the short run, at least, the outlook for the Dominican Communist party is as unpromising as at any time during the Trujillo regime.

*　*　*

In Chile the Communists appear to have brighter electoral prospects than anywhere in Latin America. The party has a disciplined and effective membership of about thirty thousand drawn primarily from miners, urban labor, students, and middle-class professionals. Even while outlawed from 1948 to 1958, the Communist Party of Chile played an active role in the coalition comprising the left-of-center Popular Action Front, placing half a dozen of its members in the Congress on the tickets of other parties. In the 1958 presidential elections the Communists vigorously supported the Popular Action Front candidate, who narrowly missed victory with 29 per cent of the votes. Campaigning under their own banner in the nationwide municipal elections in 1960, the Chilean Communists obtained nearly 10 per cent of the ballots. They bettered this record in the 1961 congressional race, garnering over 157,000 votes for 11.7 per cent of the total, to elect four senators and sixteen congressmen. Another strong Communist gain was registered in the 1963 municipal contests. From a substantially enlarged electorate the Communists attracted more than 254,000 votes—12.8 per cent of the total—to win 119 of the 1,600 municipal council posts. The unprecedented showing of the Communist party, which surpassed that of any of its partners in the Popular Action Front, has strengthened the Communists' hand in their bid to convert the Front into a Communist-oriented vehicle capable of winning the next presidential contest.

* * *

The Communist parties of Mexico and Uruguay enjoy legal standing, but neither of them now has an important following or is able to exert significant influence on national politics. The Mexican Communist Party is faction-ridden, almost completely ineffectual, and, with perhaps five thousand members, far too small to meet requirements for presenting candidates to public office. It is obliged, by default, to leave many of the tasks of the Communist movement to the Communist-front Socialist People's Party. This party, though large enough to participate in elections, is still but a minor protest group among Mexicans, who overwhelmingly feel that Marxism cannot compete with their own revolutionary heritage.

In Uruguay the Communist party has declined steadily in strength from its high of 15,000 in 1947. It now has some four thousand adherents, almost all in the capital, Montevideo. As a protest movement the Communist party can usually draw an outsized vote in national elections. In 1958, for example, the party polled 27,000 votes to elect two of its members to the National Congress. The Uruguayan Communists are highly articulate and have a well-organized, well-financed propaganda machine. However, with the most-advanced social legislation in Latin America, the Uruguayan people find little attraction in the Communist message.

* * *

The exact legal status of the Communist movement in Bolivia is unclear. Under terms of the electoral code, which denies registration to parties polling less than 4 per cent of the ballots cast in national elections, the Communists should be excluded from political activity. Nevertheless, they have participated in all national elections since 1956, even though they have failed to place any of their candidates in office or to attract as much as 2 per cent of the vote.

Bolivia is the only Latin American country in which the Trotskyist Revolutionary Workers Party compares at all favorably in size with the orthodox-Communist organization. The Trotskyist party, with about two thousand members, is perhaps half as large as the Communist Party of Bolivia. Both exert limited influence directly through propaganda and indirectly through penetration of the left wing of the National Revolutionary Movement, which has controlled the government since 1952. They compete on fairly even terms with each other, and at a distinct disadvantage with the administration party, for the support of students, the urban lower classes, and miners. Neither has been able to win a following among the Indian-peasant majority of the population.

*   *   *

The resurgence of military rule in Ecuador in July 1963 was a severe blow to the Communist movement in the country. The Communist Party of Ecuador, already badly split between rival factions in Quito and Guayaquil, was driven underground for the first time in nineteen years, and its hold on the small organized labor movement and incipient peasant organizations was at least temporarily broken. Secretary-General Pedro Saad and some two hundred leading party members were jailed, while other Communist leaders went into hiding to escape arrest. The bulk of the three thousand members—including sympathizers and hidden Communists among students and intellectuals—remained at large, but without effective organization or guidance.

*   *   *

The Communist Party of Argentina provides an excellent example of the frequent lack of correlation between numerical strength and political effectiveness among the Communist organizations of Latin America. It is the largest Communist party in the Western Hemisphere, yet it has never exerted more than marginal influence on the course of events in Argentina. The party enjoyed legal status from 1945 until 1959. In the open political climate prevailing after the overthrow of the Perón dictatorship in 1955, party membership shot up from about thirty thousand to perhaps ninety thousand, concentrated heavily in Buenos Aires and other industrial centers. The Communists polled well over 200,000 votes in the national elections of 1957 and 1958, but failed to place any of their candidates in the national or provincial legislatures, where all seats were distributed among the two leading parties. Gambling that the huge, illegal Peronist Party would make a political comeback and provide them with an entree into the government, Communists assiduously courted Peronists and cooperated closely with opportunists among them in the labor and student movements. This activity, coupled with a virulent propaganda campaign against the Frondizi administration, led the government during 1959 and 1960 to curtail Communist party operations. The Guido administration formally banned the party and its front organizations in mid-1963. The restraints on Communist operations have resulted in a sharp drop in party membership and a serious reduction in Communist propaganda capabilities. Prior to his inauguration, however, President-elect Illía indicated his intention to recognize the Communist party, while curbing its subversive activities under existing legislation. This promise, following shortly after the introduction of proportional representation in Argentine political offices, has encouraged Communist leaders to believe that they can rebuild their former mass following and that, for the first time, the Communist party may win and occupy political positions commensurate with the size and importance of its membership.

*   *   *

In 1963 the Communists in Brazil were among those who had fallen on evil times, and responsibility for their plight appeared to lie as much with the party itself as with the "objective conditions" of Brazil, which they discussed endlessly. Once clearly the leading communist organization in the hemisphere, with a membership of 150,000 and an electoral following of over half a million, the party had shrunk in a decade and a half to fewer than 40,000 members. Despite being outlawed since 1947, the party continued to enjoy all the benefits of legality except the right to present candidates to public office under its own name. It operated openly in the political sphere, allying at one time or another with every organization in the kaleidoscope of Brazilian political parties. It vigorously supported, and claimed credit for inspiring, every nationalistic achievement in the past dozen years, from the establishment of the Brazilian petroleum monopoly, *Petrobrás,* in 1953, to the nationalization of American-owned telephone companies in 1962. Its press and front organizations carried on their activities openly, but were dwindling because of waning public interest. By backing a series of losing candidates in key elections since 1958, the Communists had disproved the formerly accepted assertion that their support was essential for political victory in Brazil. Realization that Communist strength had declined seems to have made the noncommunist parties more selective in accepting Communist overtures for electoral coalitions. The major problem for the Brazilian Communists, however, was their own inability, in a period of widespread sociopolitical ferment, to present themselves convincingly as more revolutionary than the noncommunist parties. These all claim to be highly nationalistic, and virtually all of them have leaders who outdo the Communists in mouthing ultranationalistic phrases, calling for drastic socioeconomic reforms and competing for the allegiance of the urban lower and middle classes.

The Communists, of course, attributed their decline to other factors. The main stream of the Brazilian Communist movement, under the leadership of Luiz Carlos Prestes, tended to regard the party's illegal status as a major obstacle to its quest for power, and to feel that restoration of legal standing would permit it to achieve its objectives by constitutional means. Therefore, Communist spokesmen consistently denounced the proscription of the party—on the grounds that it is a branch of an international political movement—as unjust and unconstitutional. At the same time they repeatedly sought to register the party under other names. In the continuing effort to circumvent the ban against registration of international political entities in Brazil, the name of the party was formally changed to Brazilian Communist Party, on the specious argument that the new title was somehow more "national" than the original name, Communist Party of Brazil.

The latter title was appropriated by a dissident minority of less than one thousand members. The leaders of the minority party—all "old" Communists—claimed to represent the real Communist movement in the country. They attributed the failure of the movement to Prestes' leadership and rejected his espousal of a "peaceful road to socialism" in Brazil. Insisting that Communists could come to power in Brazil only by revolution, they demanded a bolder strategy and more aggressive tactics to exploit popular unrest.

Despite their differences in approach, both Brazilian Communist groups were pinning their hopes largely on the Northeast, which contained many of the ingredients for a Cuban-style revolution. These included millions of land-hungry peasants who were becoming politically active, a charismatic leader who had led the peasants to expect immediate, far-reaching agrarian reform, and a regional Communist organization which commanded several strategic positions in state and municipal governments. But even under these favorable conditions the Communists had not been able to attract a large following in the region or, by their own efforts, to ignite the popular explosion that might permit them to come to power. They were focussing a great deal of attention on Francisco Julião, the controversial leader of the peasant leagues, who had earned a nationwide reputation as spokesman for much of the rural proletariat. Under the circumstances the Communists advocated an alliance of all "progressive forces" behind the peasant movement, for their prospects for gaining power hinged in large part on their ability to make Julião and lesser peasant leaders dependent on Communist party support. The Prestes faction was apparently content to convert the peasant bodies into a vast procommunist pressure group or electoral machine. The dissident faction was seeking to transform them into a popular army under Communist control. Meanwhile, the Communist party structure remained substantially intact throughout Brazil to provide the basis for a powerful Communist apparatus if either strategy should prove successful.

* * *

The Peruvian Communist Party, with some seven thousand members, plays an active but minor role in national politics despite the legal ban on its activities since 1948. The Communists in Peru, whose capacity to incite local violence was demonstrated in the anti-Nixon riots in 1958, have never attracted a truly mass following in their own right. They have long benefited, however, from the tolerance—and at times the quiet cooperation—of Peruvian conservatives, who regard them as a lesser threat than the radical noncommunist APRA (American Popular Revolutionary Alliance) led by Víctor Raúl Haya de la Torre. Moreover, anti-APRA parties of the center and left have seldom rejected Communist support against their common rival. Under the circumstances Communists have penetrated the lower echelons of President Belaúnde's party of Popular Action and have been permitted to retain much of their influence in the labor and student movements established initially during periods of right-wing dictatorship in Peru. Although the Communist party, as such, was barred from participation in the 1963 presidential elections, the Communists claim to have provided Belaúnde's slim margin of victory. With perhaps twenty members and sympathizers in the Congress under other party labels, the Communists hope to make the administration dependent upon their support and to derive credit for the social reforms Belaúnde has promised to enact. Meanwhile, the party is persisting in its efforts to extend Communist influence to the peasant masses in order to intensify pressure on the regime for immediate and drastic agrarian reform.

* * *

The Paraguayan Communist Party is the smallest in South America and appears to have no chance to gain power except by revolution. Illegal and suppressed for more than a quarter of a century, the party has no open organization within the country. Perhaps half of its five hundred members are in exile in neighboring republics. Yet, a few Communists hold minor positions in the political, educational, and labor organizations, and the Secretary-General of the party manages to slip in and out of the country with apparent ease. The Communists played a minor part in the unsuccessful attempts to overthrow the government by revolt and invasion in 1959 and 1960.

*   *   *

Communist parties exist in each of the Central American republics and Panama, but they are uniformly small and illegal, with their leadership in exile, in hiding, or under surveillance by the government. They range in size from perhaps two thousand members in Honduras to under two hundred in Panama. The Communist Guatemalan Labor Party—shattered in 1954— was inspired by the Cuban revolution to rebuild part of its organization and to direct a wave of propaganda and violence against the Ydígoras administration. The party suffered a new setback, however, with the ouster of Ydígoras and the introduction of a military regime in 1963.

The Communists in El Salvador emerged into the open with the overthrow of the Lemus government in late 1960, attempting to foment an agrarian revolution patterned on the Cuban model. Their activities were quickly suppressed by the civilian-military directorate which took control of the government early in 1961. The Rivera administration is continuing the directorate's anti-communist policy.

The Honduran Communists, who organized a formal party most recently in 1958, are meeting only limited success in their efforts to attract support for Cuban-style revolution among students and intellectuals in the capital and among laborers on the northern banana coast.

In Nicaragua, Communist prospects depend largely upon

elimination of the Somoza machine, which continues to dominate national politics. The Nicaraguan Socialist Party—the Communist political organization—exerts some influence among other opposition groups both within the country and abroad. Exiled Nicaraguan Communists took part in the abortive Cuban-based invasion of their homeland in 1959 and continue to rely upon Cuban backing in their attempts to overthrow the regime by force.

The Communist Popular Vanguard Party in Costa Rica enjoys somewhat greater freedom of action than do its counterparts elsewhere in Central America. Barred from presenting its own candidates for public office, it nevertheless participates in national politics in support of the campaigns of other parties. Its press and front organizations function with only occasional interference by the government. The party's popular appeal, however, has diminished greatly since the emergence of José Figueres' noncommunist leftist Liberation Party as an important force in national affairs in the late 1940's. The Panamanian Party of the People, never a significant factor in the isthmian republic, has lost much of its former following and influence since being outlawed in 1953.

* * *

Communism has never exerted a significant attraction in Haiti, where the development of party organizations of any kind is still in a rudimentary stage. Nevertheless, a handful of "Marxist" intellectuals—survivors of tiny Communist parties which existed during brief flurries of open political activity in the 1930's and 1940's—are active in the government bureaucracy, and in recent years two small parties which may be regarded as Communist have emerged. These are the Party of Popular Accord, allegedly founded by Jacques Stephen Alexis in 1959 but not active until 1961, and the People's National Liberation Party, which appeared in 1961 under the leadership of Roger Gaillard. Both parties seek Soviet recognition, and they compete for support among secondary-school and university students and urban labor. The People's National Liberation Party claims to have a nationwide cell structure including peasant members. The Haitian Communists appear to have no direct links with the anti-Duvalier guerrilla movement nor sufficient strength by themselves to pose a serious threat to the government. While their ideological level is low, the existence of the two rival parties provides the nucleus of a politico-administrative apparatus which could eventually become effective in the absence of other organized opposition groups or under a regime disposed to accept large-scale international Communist support.

*   *   *

It is evident that, *by themselves,* the Communists are too few in numbers to seize power by force and far too limited in electoral following to gain power by constitutional means in any country in Latin America. Not even in Cuba is the Communist party yet strong enough to rule openly and in its own name. In Chile, where their attraction to the electorate is greatest, the Communists can realistically hope for nothing more than to be included in a coalition government presided over by the leader of another party. The aspirations of the weaker Communist parties to play a decisive role in national politics would appear to be groundless. The self-confidence of the Latin American Communists obviously cannot be explained in terms of their numbers or their ability to elect party leaders to high public office.

The optimism of the Communists stems from sources of strength outside the parties themselves, from their interpretation of the causes and course of the sociopolitical ferment that is sweeping Latin America, and from the impact of events taking place outside the hemisphere.

Nowhere in Latin America do the Communists now expect, or seek, to attain political power by their own efforts. The consolidation of supreme power in the hands of the Communist party remains their ultimate goal, but for the present and indefinite future they are content to work for more limited objectives. Past Communist efforts to go it alone in Latin America invariably failed, and the parties are now under strict instructions to avoid such a "sectarian" policy. They are now operating

under broad directives which were spelled out at the meeting
of Latin American Communists in Moscow in 1957 and repeated
periodically since. These call for the Communists to subordinate
their partisan ambition for power. They are to identify themselves with popular and national aspirations and to cooperate
with all "progressive" forces working for the elimination of
"Yankee imperialism and the vestiges of feudalism" in each of
their countries. In carrying out these directives, the various
Communist parties have adapted their tactics to fit the peculi-
arities of the national scene, ranging from wholehearted support
of the regime in Cuba to virulent opposition and subversion
against the government in Venezuela. But regardless of their
public position, the Communists everywhere outside of Cuba
have made, or are attempting to make, effective alliances with
noncommunist revolutionary forces seeking to gain power as
"democratic governments of national liberation." In the Communist lexicon such governments are an intermediate stage in
the transition from bourgeois democracy to a people's republic.
The Communists would be included as only one of several political groups in such governments.

In order to achieve these alliances, the Communists must be
able to convince the leaders of noncommunist political groups
that they command impressive resources in addition to their
limited party membership. Thus, in line with current directives
they are intensifying their efforts to build large popular followings outside of the party. They have long focused on organized
labor and the student movement as prime targets and are now
concentrating increasingly on the rural masses. Where conditions
permit they are also making a serious bid to expand their electoral support. They control the central labor confederations of
Cuba and Chile and exert a strong influence on the labor organizations of at least half the other Latin American republics. The
Communists are an important, and sometimes dominant, segment
of the university-student organizations which wield inordinate
influence in national politics in most of Latin America. Communist influence in the rural areas, which was virtually non-
existent a decade ago, is now evident in half a dozen countries.

In national elections the Communist parties of Chile, Argentina, and Venezuela have demonstrated their ability to attract a large popular vote, while those parties long barred from presenting their own candidates insist that in free elections they would now receive more ballots than ever in the past. Although the Communists consistently exaggerate their claims of public support in order to improve their political bargaining power, their influence among mass organizations is indeed widespread and appears to be on the rise in much of the area. This situation both enhances the attractiveness of the Communists as political allies and contributes to their confidence in inevitable victory.

The revolution of rising expectations which has swept over Latin America in recent years has given the Communists reason to believe that the day of victory for their cause is close at hand. The peoples of Latin America are displaying growing impatience with the traditional order and are demanding a rapid improvement in their way of life. They have made it clear that they will no longer tolerate a rigid social structure in which the great bulk of the people exists at or near the subsistence level while a small minority enjoys the cultural and material benefits of modern civilization. At the same time, the postwar population explosion, which has given Latin America the highest rate of growth in the entire world, demands unprecedented expansion of the economy merely to prevent a decline in present living levels. Under the circumstances popular aspirations have invariably been frustrated, and parties in and out of power have resorted to ever more demagogic appeals in order to retain or attract mass support. In the past few years demands for "economic independence," "industrialization," and, more recently "agrarian reform," have become the common property of virtually all significant political parties in Latin America. Governments are increasingly prone to experiment with the economic structure, while the radical opposition insists that the plight of the masses cannot be satisfactorily improved without a drastic reordering of the political and social systems as well.

The Communists interpret this wave of unrest as an extension of the postwar awakening of depressed peoples, which has led to the collapse of colonial empires in Asia and Africa and which must, in their view, inevitably lead to the establishment of Communist regimes throughout the world. They are convinced that the "imperialist camp," led by the United States, is on the defensive and that the hold of "Yankee colonialism" on Latin America can be broken. Thus, they are increasingly vocal in identifying themselves as ardent nationalists, in exaggerating and calling for immediate satisfaction of popular grievances, and in maintaining that the foreign and domestic enemies of communism are enemies of the people.

The power of the Soviet Union and the policies of the Soviet government are the major sources of the confidence of the Latin American Communists. Not only do they receive vital moral and material assistance from the U.S.S.R. and its satellites, but they are convinced that Soviet military might has seriously limited United States freedom of action in Latin America. Since 1955, when the Soviet Union launched its economic offensive among the underdeveloped nations, the Communists have incorporated Soviet trade and aid overtures as important aspects of their propaganda campaigns. They were jubilant with the success of the first sputnik in 1957, for it not only marked a major Soviet advance over the United States in the military field but demonstrated clearly that communist technology was second to none. Since that time they have registered significant success in presenting the socialist camp as a real alternative source of technical assistance, and they have pointed to the vast material progress of the Soviet Union as proof that communism provides a sure blueprint for economic development in the twentieth century. Above all, the massive Soviet-bloc aid to Cuba assures the Communists that regimes hostile to the United States and friendly to communism can survive in the Western Hemisphere.

The Political Heritage

THE ADVANCES OF COMMUNISM IN LATIN AMERICA RAISE PERPLEXING
questions and cast doubt on the validity of some widely held
assumptions about the area and its people. Latin America has
long been regarded as a bastion of Roman Catholicism and as
perhaps the last redoubt of the rugged individualist in our day.
Certainly, for more than four centuries the overwhelming majority of the people of Latin America have been Roman Catholic
in their faith. Their culture reflects the deep and continuing
influence of the Church in their lives and places great stress on
the importance of the individual in society. Moreover, the
present generation of Latin Americans is caught up in a frenzy
of nationalism which rejects foreign domination or tutelage in
any form. These qualities have been complacently cited as proof
that Latin America must remain a barren field for communism.
How, then, to account for the success of the Communist appeal
in Latin America? What does communism offer, or seem to offer,
that many Latin Americans find attractive? What is there in the
heritage and present situation of the people of Latin America
that permits them to accept or tolerate this alien, atheistic doctrine?

Some understanding of this seeming paradox can be gleaned
from a review of the Latin American past and from an examination of the basic values and goals of contemporary Latin American society. In both areas a variety of factors coincide to reduce
Latin America's much vaunted immunity to the lures of communism. This chapter reviews some of the elements in the evolution of Latin American political thought and practice that have

23

contributed to the growth of the Communist movement in recent years.

The introduction of institutions and political doctrines from abroad is not novel in Latin America. Since its discovery by Columbus nearly five centuries ago, Latin America has been in many respects an extension of Europe. Its culture is largely a composite of attitudes and institutions borrowed from other parts of the European world and modified in the Latin American milieu. To all intents and purposes Latin America has no political beliefs, concepts, or doctrines peculiar to itself.[1] None of the pre-Columbian Indian civilizations or their political systems has survived intact, and since the sixteenth century the political and intellectual leaders of Latin America have most often looked elsewhere for new ideas and inspiration.

The educated elite in Latin America has usually managed to keep abreast of contemporary developments in the centers of European thought, from the religious controversies of the sixteenth and seventeenth centuries to twentieth-century fascism and communism. In most instances the bulk of the population has been untouched by such currents of intellectual ferment, but every important political or philosophical innovation to stir the European community in the past four centuries has attracted at least a few adherents in Latin America. On those occasions when Latin Americans have drawn liberally from political systems developed in other parts of the European world, they have tended to take the most "modern" and "progressive" experiments of the day as their models.

The most far-reaching and dramatic introduction of foreign ways into Latin America occurred with the conquest, when Spaniards and Portuguese imposed the political, religious, and social institutions then dominant in Latin Europe. Eventually, in modified form, these institutions touched all segments of the

---

1. Even the apparent exceptions to this rule, the political system of modern Mexico and the ideologically based Aprista parties of Peru, Bolivia, Venezuela, and Costa Rica are largely Latin American adaptations of institutions and ideas borrowed from Europe.

native population and provided the basis for much of Latin American civilization as we know it.

During the long politico-religious conflict between Catholic and Protestant Europe, Latin America served as a battleground in the struggle for empire. Spain's rivals were able to seize a portion of its holdings in the Western Hemisphere, but then, as now, the various Protestant creeds held little attraction for the great majority of the Latin American people.

The intellectuals of Latin America followed closely and with great interest the exciting currents of thought and opinion explored in the Enlightenment of eighteenth-century France. They read and discussed treatises on the new and "scientific" discoveries of the laws of Nature and on the nature of society. They were as quick as their contemporaries in British North America to appreciate the political implications of "self-evident" truths about the inherent equality and unalienable rights of man. But even after revolution in the British colonies and in France gave political meaning to these concepts, only a tiny handful of visionaries were inspired by them to advocate a similar revolution in the Iberian colonies. Not until 1810, when immediate and practical considerations caused the leaders of Latin America to call for political independence, did these concepts find wide acceptance throughout the area. Then, they were seized upon to justify Latin America's revolt against the despotism of the Old World.

The propensity of Latin American leaders to borrow the most recent ideas and institutions from the European community was clearly demonstrated during and after the prolonged wars for independence. Nearly everywhere the traditional concept of monarchy was rejected and the radically new institution, the democratic republic, was substituted in its place. Since the Church and a highly centralized State were symbols of the old order, French anticlericalism and North American federalism became fashionable among the revolutionaries. Written constitutions, copied more or less directly from that of the United States, were the order of the day. Political parties, usually bearing the Liberal and Conservative labels of the European models that had inspired them, sprang up everywhere. Other "modern" features from the French and British political systems were adopted by one or another of the newly independent Latin American nations. Invariably, the new devices had to be drastically modified to fit the political realities of the new republics, and in most instances little remained of them except the name and the external form. But their adoption, if only in form, satisfied many proponents of change in Latin America that the new nations were up-to-date and "progressive."

After independence had been won, the educated minority in Latin America continued to seek foreign remedies to the problems of the area. During the nineteenth century both the proponents of change and the advocates of stability were eclectic in choosing from the bewildering array of doctrines, philosophies, and practices current in other parts of the European world. Among those which had a widespread and reasonably lasting impact in Latin America were the laissez-faire doctrines of British liberalism and the doctrine of political order and economic progress found in the Positivism of Auguste Comte. Before the end of the century laissez-faire economics prevailed throughout Latin America, while men dedicated to positivist ideals held key positions in the governments of Brazil and Mexico and exerted strong influence in several other Latin American countries. Both economic liberalism and Positivism have long since been rejected by the great majority in Latin America, but some ardent conservatives still urge a return to free trade and positivist arguments are still used to justify dictatorships. Moreover, the positivist concept that material progress is more important than political freedom persists in some Latin American sectors, enhancing the appeal of Communist proposals for rapid economic growth.

The Latin American intelligentsia were also attracted to the new social doctrines and philosophies current in Europe during the last century. Some were early intrigued by utopian socialism, and for a time the philosophy of Saint-Simon, in particular, was fashionable in Latin American literary circles. The interest of the intellectuals in social questions was intensified by the wave of revolutions that swept over Europe in 1848. They read and discussed virtually every social and political tract that emerged from that year of conflict. Among these was the *Communist Manifesto* written by Karl Marx and Friedrich Engels. But neither in 1848 nor for many years thereafter did the Marxist call for social justice through the class struggle find a significant response in Latin America, where the society was remarkably free of class consciousness. Marxism and other social doctrines concerned with the plight of the common man remained intellectual curiosities in Latin America until near the end of the nineteenth century.

In the four decades before World War I, Latin America not only continued to look abroad for the latest in thought and opinion, but it borrowed capital in unprecedented amounts and imported labor on a scale surpassed only by the United States. During those years hundreds of millions of pounds sterling, francs, marks, and dollars flowed into the economy of Latin America and millions of European farmers, workers, and their families poured into the temperate regions of South America. This massive influx of new money and manpower had immediate economic and social repercussions, and the political consequences were not long delayed. Railroads were built, mining flourished, new lands were opened, new industries were established, cities burgeoned, and radical ideas took root. In the larger cities the immigrant stream from Europe merged with the flow of migrants from the hinterland to create, for the first time in Latin America, a vocal, largely literate urban proletariat receptive to the appeals of radical socialism. Within a single generation, and in some countries within a decade, ideologically oriented trade unions and Socialist political parties were established. The radical sociopolitical concepts moved from the salons of the literati to political rallies in the streets of Latin America.

The radical doctrines spread quickly in the cities that absorbed the largest contingents of immigrants from southern Europe, for these immigrants were already familiar with the teachings and organizational techniques of Marxist socialism, anarchism, and syndicalism. Nevertheless, before World War I, these doctrines and methods had also made their appearance in Latin American countries that received few, if any, immigrants.

For example, Cuban revolutionaries in the 1890's and Mexican revolutionaries in the first decade of this century disseminated Marxist and anarchosyndicalist concepts they had picked up in the United States. For many years the radical movement in the United States was the usual immediate source of such European influences for the radicals of Mexico and the Caribbean.

Before the first world war, educated Latin Americans generally assumed that the area must indefinitely remain dependent upon the older, industrial nations of the Western world for both its culture and its material progress. This assumption was implicit in the choice of many of the items and ideas they imported from abroad. But the impact of world war and catastrophic world depression in this century caused them to reverse their opinion. By 1930, men reared on the doctrine of free trade and of the international division of labor had found that major dislocations of the economies and interruptions in the normal trading patterns of the industrial nations brought immediate and severe repercussions in Latin America. In such times of stress the area's exports could not be sold nor could foreign manufactured goods be imported in adequate amounts. In place of pride in their ability to produce enormous quantities of raw materials for the industries of Europe and the United States, the Latin Americans came to feel that their condition as producers of raw products and importers of finished goods was a curse that must be lifted. Under such powerful pressures economic nationalism spread widely throughout the area during the depression decade. It soon became the irresistible rallying cry of political groups of all colors, who carried it to the general public and placed it in a broad sociopolitical context. In the past few decades nationalism, with strong antiforeign overtones, has become the most apparent common denominator of Latin American political thought and action.

Much of this nationalistic fervor and activity was directed against the United States and large Yankee concerns operating in Latin America and, to a lesser extent, against their European counterparts. Yet, under the impact of the Great Depression the rising level of nationalism went hand in hand with continued dependence upon foreign sources for assistance and example. Almost without exception Latin American political parties and governments in the 1930's couched their platforms and programs in highly nationalistic terms and called for the emancipation of their countries from foreign economic domination. Thus, the evident need for Latin America to find economic security in an insecure world was expressed as a demand that Latin America gain its "economic independence" from the industrial powers, above all from the United States. At the same time the decade of the 1930's witnessed a brilliant array of testaments to the growing "interdependence" of all of the republics of the Western Hemisphere. The most insistent demand was for "national" industries to provide employment, prosperity, and protection against the calamities that might befall the United States and Europe. Foreign companies were most often expected to establish such industries. Many nationalists maintained that natural resources should be fully controlled by the state, for the benefit of the people, and even moderates insisted that the nation obtain a larger share of the proceeds of mines and fields exploited by foreign concerns. But even the government of Mexico, which expropriated vast agricultural lands owned by foreign citizens and nationalized the petroleum industry, at the expense of Yankee and European oil companies, expected private foreign companies to increase their investments in the country. While decrying Latin America's economic dependence upon the sale of a few raw material products and insisting upon the need for diversification of exports, nationalists asserted Latin America's right to tariff concessions, a protected market, and higher prices for a rising volume of its traditional exports to the United States. The emphasis was placed on Latin America's need to become self-sufficient and self-reliant, but there was little consistency in the means advocated or pursued for achieving these goals.

In the atmosphere of confusion and doubt in the 1930's a large minority in Latin America was attracted to the concept of the total state as it was emerging in Europe and the Soviet Union. Fascism and communism, with their totalitarian ideologies, powerful central regimes, rigidly controlled economies, and mass party bases, seemed to provide the answer for those who felt that Latin America lacked organization and a sense of direction. Each was hailed by its proponents as an infallible system which would give the Latin American republics social stability, economic independence, and real political sovereignty. Extremists of the Right, who felt that democracy had failed or could never succeed in Latin America, tended to favor fascism, while many who found communism desirable did so because it seemed to promise greater democracy than Latin America had ever known.

* * *

The unique contribution of twentieth-century totalitarianism to Latin America was political parties which not only drew inspiration from a foreign doctrine but identified themselves with a foreign power or bloc. Communist parties existed in most of the republics, and neo-Fascist parties, sporting distinctive shirts of red, gold, green, or other hues, arose in Cuba, Mexico, and much of South America. Although both types of parties attempted to maintain the fiction that they were fully autonomous, national organizations within an international movement, it was an open secret that they received instructions, supervision, and material support from their foreign sponsors. The Communists, without exception, sought to further the foreign-policy objectives of the Soviet Union, while the fortunes of the neo-Fascist parties were tied to those of Italy, Spain, and Nazi Germany. Each of the two opposing factions presented its system as the political system of the future and called upon the governments and people of Latin America to join the winning side. Each asserted its right to participate in the government. Both regarded such participation as the first step on the road to exclusive power. And, in Brazil, when their offers were rebuffed, both tried and failed to seize power by force. Throughout Latin America, where they existed side by side, Fascists and Communists exhausted a great deal of their energies in fighting each other. In most of the republics their use of violence eventually aroused the hostility of the government. By 1939, when communism and fascism reached a temporary accommodation in Europe, their forces in Latin America were too depleted to make a decisive joint assault on the seats of power.

In the decade before World War II fascism appeared to have a decided advantage over communism in Latin America. It attracted somewhat larger followings, particularly in Brazil, Argentina, and Chile, where there were large German minorities. It appealed more strongly than communism to men in power or close to power in several of the republics. The Fascist system, at least as practiced in Italy and on the Iberian peninsula, seemed to fall well within the Latin Catholic authoritarian tradition and to be easily adaptable to Latin America.

But it was the economic and military might of the Axis Powers even more than the ideological appeal of Fascist doctrine which accounted for the spread of fascism in Latin America. The evident success of the Axis nations in overcoming problems of unemployment and economic production impressed many who might have had reservations about the repression of political liberties under fascism. The thriving economies of Germany and Italy provided growing markets for Latin American exports at a time when the great democracies were still suffering from economic depression. Officers of the Latin American armed forces, in particular, were deeply impressed by the expanding military power of Germany and Italy, who seemed destined to dominate the Western world. Many of them urged their governments to avoid unnecessary anti-Fascist postures, some participated personally in neo-Fascist political organizations, and a few remained decidedly pro-Axis in their views until after the tide of battle turned against Germany and Italy in World War II.

Organized Fascist activities in Latin America came to an end with the defeat of the Axis in World War II. Even before the American republics were drawn into the conflict, nearly all of them had decided that their fate lay with the democracies and had initiated firm measures against groups with German or Italian backing. After Pearl Harbor the remaining pro-Axis organizations were suppressed—although in Argentina this action was delayed until 1945—and Fascist slogans disappeared from the vocabulary of politicians seeking popular support.

During World War II, as the appeal of fascism waned, Communist prestige rose sharply in Latin America. The various Communist parties, which had split off from the broad Socialist movement after the first world war and had spent most of their existence underground or on the fringes of national politics, now became respectable. After the German invasion of Russia brought the Soviet Union into the Allied camp in mid-1941, the Latin American Communists appeared as the most outspoken defenders of the democracies. Their recent ineffectual efforts to cooperate with local Fascists were soon forgotten as they called for subordination of all partisan goals for the duration of the war, support of incumbent regimes in Latin America, and complete cooperation of all democratic forces in the war against the common enemy. They continued to advocate advanced social-welfare measures, but insisted that, in the national interest, these must wait until the war was won. In these circumstances Communist objectives became virtually indistinguishable from those of truly democratic parties, which accepted Communists as allies on a far-wider scale than ever before. The party obtained legal status, often under another name, in nearly half of the republics before the end of the war, and even where it remained formally outlawed, Communists were allowed considerable freedom of action by governments which welcomed their assistance in keeping popular demands and labor unrest to a minimum.

The greatest asset of the Latin American Communists in their bid for respectability and popular acceptance was the favorable attitude toward the Soviet Union that developed during the war years. The heroic resistance of the Soviet people captured the imagination of informed Latin Americans everywhere, while the previously unsuspected military power of the Soviet Union caused them to look upon that country and the local exponents of communism with new respect. This attitude and the prestige of the Latin American Communist parties were further enhanced by actions such as the formal dissolution of the Communist International (Comintern), which led Latin Americans to believe that the Soviet Union no longer encouraged world revolution, and by the propaganda efforts of the Soviet Union and its major allies to portray Soviet communism as a variant of democracy. The Soviet Union came to be regarded as a distant, powerful, and friendly giant among nations disposed to cooperate with free nations everywhere for the betterment of mankind. By extension, the Latin American Communists were viewed as primarily nationalists, basically democratic, and seeking, like members of other parties, to increase their influence by peaceful, constitutional means.

* * *

Communist atheism would seem to raise an insurmountable barrier between the Communists and the vast Roman Catholic majority in Latin America. However, only the extremely devout found the religious issue a significant bar to the appeal or acceptance of communism. This situation reflected both the lack of deep religious conviction on the part of many nominal Catholics and the persistence of anticlericalism which developed throughout Latin America in the last century. After the long and bitter conflict which removed the Church from politics, most active Catholics came to observe a sharp separation between their religious practices and their political activities. At the same time the Communists forestalled a good deal of Catholic criticism by denying repeatedly that they sought in any way to interfere with the personal religious beliefs of the public or even of party members. Rank-and-file Communists were free to follow their own inclinations in religious matters. In recruitment campaigns the Communists insisted to prospective members that there was no conflict between membership in the party and loyalty to the Church. On occasion top Communists made a show of attending religious ceremonies as proof that even they did not have to abandon their faith to remain in good standing with international Communist leadership. The coincidence of these factors accounted in large part for the fact that communism was able to make important inroads in an area usually regarded as a stronghold of the Roman Catholic Church.

*   *   *

The acceptance and respectability of communism in Latin America reached a peak in the years between 1944 and 1947. This was a period when democracy seemed to be gaining strength throughout the area, as "liberal" administrations replaced authoritarian regimes in nine republics and dictatorial controls were temporarily relaxed in at least three others. During these years the Communist parties generally were in a stronger position than they had ever enjoyed in Latin America and their over-all membership soared to heights they have since been unable to equal. A total of perhaps 375,000 persons joined the Communist ranks, while a larger number willingly endorsed Communist causes and cast ballots for Communist candidates. The parties polled an aggregate of well over a million votes to elect Communists to local, state, or national offices in more than half of the twenty republics. For a time in Cuba, Ecuador, and later in Chile, Communists were actually appointed to cabinet positions and participated in the formulation of government policies.

The Communists attracted following and support both for what they promised and for what they could deliver. Many of the new adherents and sympathizers—perhaps a majority—were drawn to the Communist parties because their programs seemed to promise fulfillment in Latin America of the popular aspirations for a better life and personal and political liberties that figured so prominently among the war aims of the Allies. Many others were attracted by the real power and influence the Communists had built up in the wartime climate of tolerance and cooperation. Communists had gained control of the Confederation of Latin American Workers, had taken over the central labor organization of Cuba, and were a force to contend with in the labor movement of nearly every other country of the area. Their electoral following was highly impressive and their influence in most of the governments of Latin America was a recognized fact. They were in a position to cause a great deal of trouble for selected enemies and to grant important favors for friends of the party. Some persons joined the party because it was on the rise and opened prospects for personal advancement. Employers who wanted to avoid labor difficulties found it convenient to contribute to party coffers. And politicians in need of votes sought Communist support in exchange for future collaboration which would further enhance the influence and prestige of the party.

With the advent of the cold war in 1947, Communist fortunes declined as rapidly as they had risen. The Communists found that close identification with the Soviet Union, until recently an asset, was now a distinct liability which left them vulnerable to suspicion and attack by their wartime allies. Their sudden switch from praise to violent denunciation of the United States and its friends in Latin America, even before the wartime passion for inter-American cooperation had begun to cool, caused informed Latin Americans to question Communist sincerity and motives. In a period of rising nationalism, which the Communists had encouraged, their efforts to portray themselves as ardent nationalists were badly undercut by Soviet insistence that party leaders publicly reiterate their overriding loyalty to Moscow. Their pose as democrats was weakened by liberals and noncommunist leftists who cited the Communists' frequent collaboration with dictators in public charges against them.

These tactical blunders and embarrassing revelations, however, were not in themselves sufficient to account for the sharp drop in Communist prestige after 1947. This resulted primarily from the actions of political adversaries and hostile governments which destroyed the respectability of the party, cut into the sources of Communist strength, and appeared to eliminate Communist political influence in most of Latin America. While the Communists were still riding high, the noncommunists, free from the wartime pressure to cooperate for a common end, had resumed the open contest for control of labor and student organizations and for electoral support. By 1948 noncommunist parties from Cuba to Chile had wrested control of labor from the Communists and were challenging their hold on youth, student, and intellectual circles. In several countries this competition was encouraged by the "liberal" regimes that had come to power in the immediate postwar period. Even where such regimes did not survive, successor governments generally continued an anti-communist policy. Before the end of 1948 the Communist movement had again been outlawed in eight of the republics. By 1956 most Communists had been removed from public office, the party had been stricken from the electoral lists, and Communist propaganda outlets had been closed or restricted in fourteen of the twenty countries. Over-all Communist party membership did not greatly exceed 200,000 for all of Latin America, and in some countries for all practical purposes the party had ceased to exist.

Only in Guatemala, where the party sought to identify itself with a popular revolution and received the backing of a friendly government, were the Communists able temporarily to build a position of strength and influence during the postwar decade. This position was effectively destroyed when the Arbenz administration was overthrown by anticommunist forces in 1954.

The postwar anticommunist trend coincided with the resurgence of authoritarian regimes throughout much of Latin America after 1948. By 1954 there were open or lightly disguised dictatorships in a dozen Latin American countries, and in all but one of them—Perón's Argentina—the Communist party was illegal. For the dictators, however, suppression of the Communist party was only incidental to suppression of all local opposition. They proclaimed their anticommunist sentiments at every opportunity, primarily to win favor or to forestall criticism from the United States.

The postwar dictators in Latin America, like their predecessors, were far more concerned with retaining power than with supporting or opposing any political ideology. Moreover, they did not fear the numerically insignificant Communist parties. Most of them, like their predecessors, found it expedient to use Communists in their efforts to break the power of the democratic parties that posed a real threat to their survival. Since these parties also represented the more serious, lasting danger to the Communist movement, Communists became willing collaborators of dictators who had outlawed the party and jailed or exiled its top leaders. In several countries the communist party gave the appearance of splitting, with the segment loyal to the established leadership maintaining an ineffectual opposition underground or from exile, while the "dissident" branch cooperated quietly with the regime. Communist assistance was particularly valuable in curbing labor unrest among workers of food and service industries, where strikes would have an immediate impact on the general public, and among workers of the plantations, mines, and oil fields that contributed an important share of the government's income. Communists were also permitted to penetrate the communications media which heaped lavish praise on the chief of state. Thus, most of the "anticommunist" dictators not only failed to destroy the Communist party apparatus, but allowed the Communists to recover much of the organizational base they had lost to the democratic parties shortly after the war.

Under the dictatorships the Communists did not abandon their demands for social and economic "progress" to improve the lot of the masses, but subordinated them to the achievement of immediate political goals. Party leaders or the leaders of the opposition wing where the Communists had split publicly denounced the dictatorship and proclaimed the restoration of political freedom as the primary Communist objectives. In such circumstances the Communists were generally tolerated or accepted as allies by democratic opposition groups and allowed full freedom of action when political liberties were restored. The ability of the Communists to exploit contradictory currents in Latin American political tradition, simultaneously extracting aid and comfort from both dictators and democrats, accounts to a large extent for the rapid expansion of the Communist parties when the dictatorships began toppling in the mid-1950's.

THREE

The Present Appeal of Communism

THE CAPACITY OF THE LATIN AMERICAN COMMUNIST PARTIES FOR turning apparent catastrophe to advantage, as they did under most of the "anticommunist" dictatorships, explains in large measure their seeming phoenixlike quality to rise fully formed from the ashes of defeat. This phenomenon recurs throughout the history of many of the parties and is well-known to noncommunist political leaders from one end of Latin America to the other. Time after time the Communists have collaborated with former enemies in order to preserve the party so that it might fulfill its primary mission—the furtherance of current Soviet foreign-policy objectives. The dispassionate observer may understand, even if he does not condone, this Machiavellian attitude on the part of the Communists, but he is frequently at a loss to discover a logical explanation for the willingness of noncommunist groups to invite or accept Communist collaboration.

There is a great deal in the present situation of Latin America that favors the spread of communistic ideas and makes it comparatively easy for the Communists to exploit the weaknesses and ambitions of other political leaders. It is a truism that Latin America is in the throes of a great socioeconomic transition that threatens momentarily to burst into violent revolution. In this atmosphere, in which "moderates" are insisting on changes that were regarded as revolutionary only a few years ago, Communist proposals seem less radical than they might otherwise appear. Indeed, it is no small embarrassment to the Communists that so many of their views are widely accepted and have been taken over by noncommunist parties with no affinity for Moscow. Nevertheless, in this situation where Marxism is accepted by opinion molders as a respectable political philosophy, where the populace has been awakened to demand the material benefits already achieved in the Soviet Union, and where rampant nationalism disposes many Latin Americans to hostility toward the United States, the Communists are assured a large, and at times highly receptive, audience for their appeals. And the Communist parties, themselves, possess certain qualities and capabilities that permit them to elicit cooperation or tolerance from a broad sector of the Latin American public. Under these circumstances, in recent years the Communists have generally found popular support for the proposition that they are legitimate nationalistic revolutionaries, whose help is desirable in the present revolutionary situation.

Cooperation between the Communist and noncommunist parties is facilitated to a large degree by their leaders speaking the same political language. In the past half century Marxism has become part of the common background of most well-educated Latin Americans. Whether as advocates or adversaries, the university students who have gone into politics have been familiar with the basic tenets of Marxist socialism. The ideologically based, noncommunist parties—Socialist, Aprista, and to a lesser extent even the Social Christian—share with the Communists some of the fundamental assumptions about society, economics, and politics that have been carried over from nineteenth-century Marxist socialism to modern Marxism-Leninism. They are all "international" parties, in aspiration if not in fact. They are all concerned for the social and economic improvement of the masses. They all stress the importance of economic factors as determinants of political and social developments, and, to a greater or lesser degree, they accept the Marxist theory of the "inevitability" of historical trends. The demagogues who head essentially personal political organizations, and even the leaders of the traditional Liberal and Conservative parties, are well acquainted with Marxist clichés and employ them, as expedient, in their appeals for popular support. In explaining the causes of many Latin American problems, Communist and noncommunist politicians frequently build on the same theoretical base and couch their arguments in similar terms.

On the level of practical politics the similarities between the Communist and noncommunist parties appear even greater. Despite the vast differences between the ideals and ultimate goals of the two groups, they are often more like than unlike in their approach to immediate political problems. They appeal to the same groups in society in much the same terms. They seek to build the same kinds of organizational support outside of the party itself. They employ essentially the same techniques and devices in obtaining votes, and they frequently propose similar solutions to immediate national problems. Since the areas of agreement are often greater than the differences between them over methods, neither finds it necessary to modify its political practices in order to cooperate effectively with the other.

On several fundamental points the Communist political system bears a striking resemblance to the kinds of authoritarian rule that every Latin American republic has known and that are still common in parts of the region. Furthermore, on most of these points, current Communist practices appear to be compatible with the goals or inclinations of nearly all noncommunist parties. The dominant role of the state is not peculiar to Communist regimes but is accepted as a fact or a goal by most noncommunist parties. The subordination of the individual to society, or, more exactly, to the political group currently in power, has been a recurrent theme in much of Latin America's political history and has been rising since the political parties have become concerned with the masses. The goal of a one-party system, in which party and government are indivisible, was achieved by some Latin American dictators long before the rise of the Communist party in Russia, and has been the aspiration of most Latin American strong men. The concept of single-party rule, already firmly rooted in noncommunist Mexico, does not appear to be abhorrent to any important political group in Latin America, although no party would willingly submit to total domination by another. Even the dominance of an all-powerful leader, who serves in the Communist system as the infallible interpreter of truth and justice, does not differ drastically from what most Latin American republics have known under vainglorious dictators. And intolerance of opposition is certainly not restricted to communist regimes. It has been characteristic of all dictatorships and is seen in the use of the state of siege, the exiling of political enemies, and other devices employed even by "liberal" regimes in much of Latin America. Despite the volumes of glorious prose and the innumerable constitutions written in Latin America extolling the virtues of democracy and the rights of the individual, democratic rule and the full enjoyment of political and personal liberties are ideals that have yet to be realized in much of the area. Cold political reality in some parts of Latin America is still closer to communism as it is known in this century than most noncommunist leaders care to admit.

In view of these basic similarities, it is evident that the Communist political system is not incompatible with many undemocratic aspects of Latin America's political heritage. Although most noncommunist parties are seeking to overcome such aspects of their heritage and are opposed to the prospect of Communist rule, they recognize much in communism that has long been familiar to the Latin American scene. Some of them, moreover, find in communism elements which they regard as desirable. In spite of their genuine democratic aspirations, many Latin American political leaders cannot find the Communists as alien as they appear to citizens of countries where democratic processes work effectively and democratic privileges are taken for granted. Thus, cooperation with Communists is no more repugnant to most noncommunist politicians than is cooperation with other erstwhile adversaries, when their immediate interests coincide or seem to coincide.

The comparatively small size of the Communist parties frequently makes it easy for noncommunist groups to tolerate their activities or accept them as political allies. More often than not the noncommunist argument is that since the Communists are so few in number they need not be feared. This reasoning persists even though it has repeatedly been proved fallacious, most recently by events in Cuba since 1959. The noncommunist political leaders, moreover, are often acquaintances, sometimes personal friends, of the top men in the local Communist organization. They often have similar backgrounds and share similar interests. In most instances they have worked closely together at one time or another in the past. The noncommunist politician is apt to regard the political proclivities of his communist colleague as little more than harmless eccentricities. It is extremely difficult for such individuals to look upon the Communists as other than the misguided but sincere nationalists they sometimes appear to be. To date, this view is still widely held and continues to facilitate the spread of communism in Latin America.

The Communists often obtain useful support or cooperation even from their most dangerous enemies, the ideological parties of the noncommunist left in Latin America. The leaders of these parties, which advocate socioeconomic reforms with political liberties, generally realize that the Communists are unreliable allies, who consistently place Soviet interests above those of the nation and who seek ultimately to restrict rather than expand the areas of political freedom in Latin America. Where such parties have come to power or have prospects of attaining power, they suffer the full brunt of Communist propaganda attacks. Yet, the leaders of such parties usually insist that the Communists should have freedom to expound their views. Moreover, they are often unable to convince their followers of the dangers of cooperation with the Communist party, and must accept Communist collaboration or a split in their own ranks. Where these parties are weak—as in the case of most of the Socialist parties of Latin America—divisions between an anticommunist right wing and a procommunist left wing are common. Even right-wing leaders of the smaller ideological parties often persuade themselves that they can use the Communists to build a stronger position and discard them later when Communist support becomes a liability. All these circumstances provide opportunities for the Communist parties to increase their activities in Latin America.

It is one of the apparent contradictions of communism in Latin America that while communism purports to be the doctrine of the working class its appeal has usually been strongest among intellectuals and pseudointellectuals. This group has always been a prime target of the Communist movement because it occupies a prestigious and highly influential position in Latin American society. Artists, writers, newsmen, members of the professions, teachers, and students—all those with a claim to intellectual attainments—shape the political views of the electorate and exhibit interest in political activities to a much higher degree than do their counterparts in the United States. The community of intellectuals provides most of the top leadership of all Latin American political parties, including the Communist party. It provides a significant percentage of the new members drawn into the Communist party as well as a large portion of the sympathizers who support Communist causes and lend the prestige of their names to the Communist movement. The acceptance of communism by such men as Mexican painters Diego Rivera and David Alfaro Siqueiros, Brazilian novelist Jorge Amado, and the outstanding Chilean poet Pablo Neruda has contributed to the respectability of the communist party in much of Latin America.

Students in Latin America are a highly susceptible target of Communist propaganda. They constitute a privileged minority which has traditionally played an influential role in national politics. As a group they are idealists, ardent nationalists, and articulate critics of the *status quo*. They are notoriously intolerant of evolutionary approaches to solution of national problems and quick to seize upon ready-made formulas that promise simple and immediate remedies. Students, moreover, enjoy certain clear advantages in the political arena. Their views are widely respected as those of an elite group, they are usually less responsible, better organized, and easier to mobilize than other sectors of the intellectual and pseudointellectual elite, and their status as students ordinarily protects them against the consequences of rash political actions. Most Latin American governments are reluctant to use force against student demonstrations or riots. For these reasons the Communists have exerted, and continue to exert, a great deal of effort to build a following among university students, and even among pupils in secondary schools, nearly everywhere in Latin America.

In recent years the Communists have scored their greatest advances by appealing to the urgency for material improvement that is shared by the bulk of the Latin American population. They continue to appeal as well to the long-standing aspirations of informed people in much of Latin America for responsible democratic government and political liberties, but they place greatest emphasis on the social and economic expectations of the masses and on the widespread demand for "national sovereignty."

The Communists have long perceived and exploited the fact that the great majority of the Latin American populace has little interest in achieving democracy as it is known in the United States and Western Europe. Rather, the craving of the people is for a rapid improvement in the material conditions of life and for a dramatic change of social status which will recognize the inherent dignity of the individual. The masses of Latin America have demonstrated their impatience with traditional methods and their willingness to follow political leaders who promise to show them how to realize their social and economic expectations in the shortest possible time. The Communists maintain, consistently, vehemently, and with apparent sincerity, that these are precisely the goals for which they are striving. Moreover, since the victory of Castro in Cuba the Communists point to the greatly enhanced social and economic status of the Cuban peasants as proof that the kind of revolutionary regime they advocate will make good on its promises.

The Communist propaganda campaign for economic development is inextricably linked with the campaign for the establishment of "fully sovereign" governments throughout Latin America. In urging the installation of regimes that will be "independent" in foreign affairs, the Communists strike a responsive chord in nearly all patriotic Latin Americans. As self-proclaimed nationalists, the Communists define an "independent" foreign policy in the present epoch as one that is firmly opposed to alleged "imperialistic designs" of the United States on Latin America. Many Latin Americans who differ with the Communists on other issues endorse Communist demands for such a foreign policy.

It is ironic that the Communists, with their well-known international ties, should have a large measure of success in passing themselves off as dedicated nationalists. Their loyalty to the Soviet Union precludes the possibility that they can be the sincere Latin American patriots they pretend to be. This basic conflict of interests, however, is frequently ignored or overlooked by other Latin Americans because the Communists are entirely sincere, both as Latin Americans and as Communists, in encouraging the spread of hostility toward the United States. This is one of the primary tasks of the Communist party and one that is made easier by the tendency of many Latin Americans to equate anti-Yankee sentiments with patriotic nationalism. The Communists are by no means alone in exploiting this tendency, but they are more consistent than most of the noncommunist groups in insisting that a true nationalist must oppose the United States at every turn.

Paradoxically, the spread of anti-United States nationalism has been facilitated by the fact that most politically active Latin Americans have an ambivalent attitude toward this country, with mingled feelings of animosity and admiration. The dominant sentiment at any particular time is usually determined by immediate circumstances, a fact which political orators of all persuasions have learned to play upon as suits the occasion. Thus, the same audience which applauds the United States as a great friend and ally of Latin America in its quest for democracy, economic progress, and social justice will also listen sympathetically to denunciations of the United States for its past policies of intervention or more recent "neglect" of Latin America and its needs. In times of stress political parties seeking power, and even "friendly" governments as well, have found it easy and expedient to use "Yankee imperialism" as a whipping boy, placing the blame for Latin America's troubles on United States actions or lack of action. Under these circumstances it has been simple for the Communists, for many opportunists riding the wave of nationalism, and for the minority with unmixed feelings of hostility toward this country to go one step farther, tagging the United States, "Wall Street," and "Yankee trusts" in Latin America as the chief enemies and exploiters of the area and its people. In this situation it is not surprising that some anti-Yankee extremists, accepting the deceptive logic that "the enemy of my enemy is my friend," should follow Communist urging and look to the enemies of the United States for aid, comfort, and political inspiration.

Receptivity to this Communist appeal is enhanced by the widespread respect of Latin Americans for the material achievements of the Soviet Union and by their tendency to regard Soviet capabilities as greater than they are in fact. The Communists exploit this attitude by all means at their disposal, tailoring their approach to fit the interest of each audience. Although numerous other political groups also recommend closer relations between Latin America and the Communist bloc, the Communists' well-known links with the Soviet Union lend an air of authenticity to their urgings that Latin America follow the Soviet example and avail itself of the opportunity to benefit from Soviet experience. To the artists and intellectuals the Communists stress the high level of music and the arts in Soviet culture. To the sports enthusiasts they emphasize Soviet prowess in this field. To those concerned with science and technology they point to the fantastic achievements of scientists and technicians trained under Communist rule. To those resentful over Latin America's economic underdevelopment and present low rank in the hierarchy of national powers they stress the similarities between Russia in 1917 and Latin America today. They point out that the Soviet people under a Communist regime moved from the era of Cossacks to the age of sputniks in only four decades, that the Soviet Union rose from economic backwardness to super-power status in less than a single lifetime. They predict flatly that Latin America can attain the same goals, in fact, that with the added advantage of help from the Communist countries it can attain these goals in even shorter time.

Under present conditions the Communists insist that Latin America does *not* need to install Communist regimes in order to benefit from the experience and cooperation of the Soviet Union. This approach appeals to the many who believe that Latin America can adapt Soviet economic methods and tap the supposedly unlimited markets of the Communist bloc without accepting communism. The Communists maintain that the Soviet Union has no political interests in Latin America but stands ready to assist all peoples to improve their economic position and to preserve their national sovereignty. To those whose nationalism is based largely on hatred for the United States, the Communists argue that the existence of the Soviet Union makes it no longer necessary for Latin America to remain in "colonial bondage" to the Yankees. The Cuban example is cited as proof that if a Latin American republic dares to cast off the "imperialist yoke" the Communist bloc will provide the full range of economic, scientific, and cultural cooperation without political obligation. The Communists encourage Latin American nationalists generally in the conviction that, in a world dominated by two giant nations, it is not in Latin America's best interest to identify itself completely with one of these nations and to deny itself access to the experience of the other simply because that nation has a Communist political system. Though relatively few people in Latin America are yet prepared to follow all of the Communist arguments to their logical conclusion, much of the Communists' reasoning has a strong general appeal.

It is apparent that in their quest for popular acceptance and support the Communists must give, or appear to give, equal value in return. As compensation for the backing and political cooperation they seek, the Latin American Communists offer both practical and psychological, immediate and long-term rewards. To all those willing to cooperate with them, whether it be in the labor movement, in front organizations, in peasant societies, or in political alliances of shorter or longer duration, the Communists provide their organizational skills, the services of a political party with international ties, and a well-financed, generally effective propaganda apparatus. To those looking for leadership the Communists supply a program of action and a set of concrete goals for which to strive. They play upon the immediate physical and emotional needs of all major sectors of society. They explain in terms that each audience can understand the "rights" to which each is entitled, they point out the domestic and foreign "enemies" who deprive them of these "rights," and they offer an apparently infallible doctrine which shows them how to attain what is rightfully theirs.

One of the features which enhances the Communists' bargaining power with other groups is the efficiency that the party extracts through discipline over its members. The Communist party insists on and obtains strict obedience at all levels to commands issued by higher echelons. Although a semblance of the democratic process is maintained within the party, whereby members may discuss, and occasionally dispute, pending shifts in tactics, no protest is permitted once a decision has been reached at the top. Frequently there is no time for advance notice of changes in line, and all party members are expected to obey instructions without question. In this quality the Communist party is almost unique in Latin America. Throughout most of the area political-party members feel free to cross party lines, to change party affiliation, or to strike out in defiance of the national leadership to a degree surprising to those familiar with Anglo-American political practices. Unless contrived as an unusual, short-term tactic to achieve a specific objective, such disobedience in the Communist party is branded as "deviationism," and all the power the party can bring to bear is leveled against the offenders. Communist discipline, although not always enforceable, generally makes the party more effective in its day-to-day operations than noncommunist parties with larger followings. This discipline extends also to such "nonpolitical" entities as trade unions and student organizations in which Communist control is firm. When Communist leaders call upon all party members and members of Communist-dominated organizations to appear for a political rally, a street demonstration, a riot, or a strike, they can usually be confident that the members will respond as ordered.

The Communists may well feel no obligation to keep long-range commitments to other groups, but they are usually able and prompt to deliver on promises made in their own immediate interest. When they pledge cooperation in an electoral campaign, financing, or other support to a temporary political ally, or when they assure the employer of Communist-led workers that there will be no strike in his concern, they keep their word. This faculty has given the Communists an inflated reputation for honesty and efficiency that permits the party to exert political influence out of all proportion to its numbers.

For the comparatively few Latin Americans who enter the party, the Communists offer continuing psychological and material rewards. Of these the intangible benefits appear to provide the stronger incentive. Those who become Communists usually accept communism at face value, as a doctrine which will show them how to combat evil and build a better life for society. For many such individuals communism seems to supply the answers to man's eternal queries about the meaning and purpose of his existence. In communism they believe they have found a total and integrated philosophy which explains their relationship to the rest of mankind and their place in the stream of history. Many find in it an outlet for the missionary zeal they are unable or unwilling to channel through the Church. They hurl themselves into party activities with dedication, convinced that they are working on the side of right and justice and that victory must inevitably be theirs. The new Communists are excited by vicarious identification with one of the super powers of our day. They derive a sense of importance from their connection with a vast international organization and often find that as Communists they can play a more important role in national politics than they might have anticipated as members of small, indigenous protest groups.

Those who rise even to the intermediate rungs of the party hierarchy discover that the perquisites of their position are tangible indeed, frequently permitting them to mingle and deal on equal footing with men from the highest levels of society. Participation in an international movement enables them to travel, to meet with the leaders and other prominent figures of communist states abroad, to expand their horizons beyond the parochial boundaries that confine some of their noncommunist counterparts. If the party should be suppressed at home, their role in the international Communist movement assures them a safe haven in communist countries or subvention while in exile in neighboring republics.

In view of the many circumstances favorable to the communist movement, it may seem surprising that the Latin American Communists have not made even greater advances in recent years. But the very circumstances and conditions that permit the Communists to gain acceptance have served, thus far, to restrict the audiences to whom they can appeal effectively. In part, this situation is of the Communists' own making. Through their current insistence that they are virtually identical with other leftist parties, they are obliged to minimize the real differences that might attract those prepared for a complete break with the past. By maintaining that they seek only to help other groups to achieve the national revolution, they surrender part of their claim to the leadership of the masses.

A far more important limitation on Communist effectiveness lies in the existence of noncommunist parties that appear equally or more revolutionary. The people of Latin America who might be expected to respond to the Communist appeal have a wide range of choice among political parties advocating radical changes to raise living standards, to improve the social status of the lower classes, and to make their nations economically and politically sovereign. The individual seeking dramatic solutions to his country's problems can find nearly every aspect of the Communist program in the platforms of one or another of the center or leftist parties. Several of these parties, moreover, have come to power or have a much better chance than the Communists to attain power. For the great majority of the Latin Americans the noncommunist parties have the advantage of incorporating some of the "desirable" features of communism in an authentically national program.

The Alliance for Progress program has given new hope to large sectors of the informed public in Latin America that significant socioeconomic advances can be achieved without political upheaval. This new element has done a good deal to drive a wedge between the Communist and noncommunist parties and to check the spread of hostility toward the United States. However, every delay and setback encountered by the Alliance for Progress increases popular frustrations and lends credence to the Communists' charges that real progress is impossible under existing political arrangements, domestic and international. The Communists are confident that there will be enough such delays and frustrations to turn the Latin American masses solidly against the United States, to alienate them from the noncommunist parties identified with the Alliance for Progress, and to make them even more receptive to the appeal of communism.

II.

The Role of the
Communist Parties

XXXXXX FOUR XXXXXX

The Rise of the Communist Parties

IN THE HISTORY OF LATIN AMERICA THE COMMUNIST MOVEMENT appears as a recent and alien phenomenon. All the Communist parties came into being after the famous October Revolution in Russia, and only four can trace their origins to parties that existed before 1917. From its inception each of them has looked exclusively to Marxism, as interpreted by the head of the Soviet state, for its inspiration, ideology, and guidance. No Communist party has sought to draw upon Latin America's heritage of indigenous "communistic" societies or seriously to identify itself with the surviving communal practices of the descendents of Aztecs, Mayas, or Incas. The few foolhardy comrades who suggested such a course were promptly denounced as heretics, as were those who wanted the Latin American parties to interpret Marxism in national or regional terms. From the beginning the first loyalty of every Communist party has been to the Soviet Union, not to the republic in which it operates.

Two characteristics of the Latin American Communist parties have served to obscure many details surrounding their origins. First, the early Communists usually represented such an insignificant segment of the radical movement that the founding of a Communist party failed to attract special attention. Even though subsequently the Communists have often claimed that the party attracted popular support from the outset and was immediately recognized as a mortal threat by reactionary regimes, this was seldom the case. In countries where all political opposition was suspect or prohibited when a Communist party was organized, the Communists did not seek to call attention to

55

themselves. But in well over half of the republics of Latin America, where such proscriptions did not exist or were not rigidly enforced, the Communists were able to organize openly. Yet, in nearly every instance the establishment of a new Communist party, whether legal or clandestine, passed unnoticed by the general public and by the government.

Most of the parties have maintained official silence on many aspects of their past policies and actions. Party leaders generally have preferred to avoid needless embarrassment and the possible confusion of new members by publishing detailed accounts of reversals and counterreversals of earlier policies. It would be embarrassing to the present party leadership for the Peruvian Communists to reveal that José Carlos Mariátegui, whom they revere as the "Father of Communism in Peru," was denounced as a Trotskyist only a few months before his death, or for the Cuban Communists to recall that the martyr-hero of their party, Julio Antonio Mella, was on the point of expulsion from the Communist movement at the time of his assassination. It might well disturb Brazilian Communists to be reminded that in 1930 the party publicly denounced its present Secretary-General, Luiz Carlos Prestes, for advocating tactics it enthusiastically endorsed five years later. Each of the parties has comparable memories which it would rather not revive.

Under the circumstances, the Latin American Communist parties, with few exceptions, have not attempted to write their own histories, and prominent Communists have seldom indulged in the luxury of compiling their memoirs. In the few party or personal chronicles that have been published contradictory details have been omitted or distorted to indicate that the party or individual was always basically in tune with the international Communist line current at the time of publication. Thus, few Latin American Communists know much of their own party history. Those who would do so must turn either to scattered documents or to accounts prepared by anticommunists, many of whom were formerly party members.

The turbulent years from the first to the second world war witnessed the emergence of Communist parties or groups in every country of Latin America. The Communist Party of Argentina, established in 1918, has the dubious honor of being the oldest such organization in the Western Hemisphere, whereas in the Dominican Republic the Communists were not able to organize for the first time until 1942. Most of the Latin American parties have been active continuously from the date of their founding. A few have had a chaotic existence, disappearing for shorter or longer periods to be re-created two or even three times. On occasion there have been as many as three rival Communist organizations, in addition to Trotskyists, operating within a single country. Only recently, however, have there been organized Communist parties active simultaneously within all twenty of the republics.

The Latin American Communist parties appear to have come into existence by one or more of half a dozen different routes. The Chilean and Uruguayan parties were formed by the adherence of existing Socialist organizations to the Third or Communist International. Socialist minorities bolted from the parent body to create the Communist parties of Argentina and Mexico. These tactics were later used by Communists within the new Socialist parties established in Colombia, Ecuador, and Peru in the 1920's. The party in Brazil resulted from the conversion and consolidation of anarchosyndicalist groups in 1922, while some of the later parties were started by the merger of scattered Marxist "study groups" that had developed more or less spontaneously. Several parties were organized by international Communist agents, either foreigners or returning exiles who had joined the Communist movement abroad. Nearly all of them had some assistance from outside Communist sources. The Argentine and Brazilian parties are probably the only ones in Latin America that came into being without the "cooperation" of Communists from other countries. At the other extreme is the Dominican Communist Party, which appears to have formed as an outgrowth of Communist organizations established by Spanish and Catalonian exiles after the civil war in Spain.

The establishment of the Communist parties has taken place in at least five waves or phases. During the first of these, from

1918 to 1922, five parties were formed. Communist and Communist-front parties appeared in nine countries in the second period, which began about 1924 and lasted through 1928. Another three parties were added between 1929 and 1931, while existing front parties were transformed into full-fledged Communist organizations. The decade from the mid-1930's to the end of World War II witnessed the creation of three more parties, only one of which called itself Communist. During these same years half a dozen parties abandoned the Communist label without changing their political orientation. The current phase, which began about 1946, has been characterized by the revival of some older parties that had virtually ceased to exist and by occasional efforts to convert front parties into avowed Communist parties. A review of these periods reveals that each wave of Communist organizational activity corresponded to changing conditions within the various Latin American republics and to shifting exigencies of Soviet foreign policy.

THE EARLY PARTIES

The earliest and most permanent, although not always the strongest, Communist parties were organized in the countries where the industrial revolution had made the most headway and where the labor movement had begun to acquire national prominence. In these countries, Argentina, Mexico, Uruguay, Chile, and Brazil, there was a substantial audience of organized urban workers and restive intellectuals receptive to the ideas and examples provided by postwar Russia. The men who created the communist parties were excited by these ideas and examples and, except in Mexico, needed little or no additional encouragement from foreign sources to transform themselves and their followers into Communists. They adhered eagerly to the international movement. The Argentine party regarded itself as a charter member of the Comintern, which was founded in 1919, and the others were affiliated almost immediately after their formation. They all adopted names which expressly revealed that affiliation, as shown in the formal title of the Brazilian party: Communist

Party of Brazil, Brazilian Section of the Communist International.

Argentina

The first Communist organization in Argentina was formed on January 6, 1918 as the International Socialist Party. It was comprised of a group of dissidents from the older Socialist Party of Argentina. This group, which may have included as many as two thousand members, had been expelled even before the outbreak of the Russian Revolution because of its opposition to the pro-Allied stand of the Socialist party leadership. Prominent among the dissidents were Victorio Codovilla and Rodolfo Ghioldi, who have long been the dominant figures in the Argentine Communist movement. The new party hailed the successful revolutionaries in Russia as the "heroic vanguard of international socialism," and gave its proxy to the Italian Socialist party which attended the founding congress of the Comintern. In December 1920 it dropped its original name and assumed the title Communist Party of Argentina in conformity with instructions issued by the Comintern. It has retained this name continuously since that time.

The Argentine Communists enjoyed legal status until about 1925 and *de facto* freedom of operation until 1930. They failed, however, to build the party into a significant force in politics or in the labor movement. Beginning in 1918 they participated in electoral campaigns, occasionally placing two or three candidates at the municipal level. Their vote was largest in Buenos Aires, Córdoba, and Mendoza, centers which still provide the bulk of the Communist party following. Although the Communists concentrated their attention largely on the labor movement and managed to gain substantial control over the metallurgical and construction workers and over a portion of the railroad workers, they were unable to break the hold of Socialists and anarchists on the large labor federations. Persistent factionalism during its first dozen years accounted for much of the party's ineffectiveness. Numerous resignations and the expulsion of dissidents more than offset modest increases in membership by accretion from the Socialist party. It was customary at that time for Communist parties to submit to the Comintern highly inflated membership figures. The Argentine claim of 3,500 members, reported in 1922 and repeated in 1924, was no exception. In those years the party was probably little if any larger than it had been in 1918, and by the end of the decade it was even smaller.

The weak and divided Argentine party serves as an excellent standard by which to gauge the strength and effectiveness of the Communist movement in Latin America during the first decade. Throughout the 1920's the Comintern consistently looked upon the Communist Party of Argentina as its greatest achievement in the area. Subsequently the party became more cohesive and its membership increased many fold, but it has never since ranked first in importance among the Latin American parties.

In the decade and a half after 1930 the fortunes of the Argentine party alternately plummeted and soared as the Communists blindly attempted to apply contradictory Soviet directives to a rapidly changing, domestic political situation. With the *coup d'état* which overthrew the government in September 1930, the party was driven underground and its activities were severely curtailed. For about five years Communist refusal to work with other opposition groups left the party politically isolated. This situation was reversed in 1935, when the Communists adopted the popular-front policy of cooperation with "anti-Fascist" forces. Although they failed to achieve a formal alliance with other left-wing parties, the Argentine Communists increased their strength in the labor movement and attracted a fair degree of popular sympathy for their strong protests against authoritarian rule at home and the spread of fascism in Europe. Membership in the Communist party reached a new high. The party was again isolated during the interval of the Hitler-Stalin pact, but recuperated quickly when it assumed a vigorous pro-Allies stand after the Soviet Union entered the war against the Axis. Communist plans for an electoral coalition with the powerful Radical party in 1943 were upset by the armed forces, who seized power in June of that year. Once more party leaders were jailed or exiled and the Communist press was closed, while the spectacular rise of Juan Perón undercut the Communist position in the labor movement. But the party survived to extract maximum advantage from the defeat of the Axis and the last-minute switch of Argentina to the democratic camp. When political liberties were restored in 1945, the Communist party was granted legal status. Operating without restraints for the first time in two decades, it rose to some thirty thousand members and polled more than 150,000 votes in the national elections of February 1946. Communist strength remained at about this level through the years of the Perón era.

Mexico

The Mexican Revolution, which began in 1910 and persisted as a violent social and political upheaval for a full decade, provided innumerable opportunities for those who wanted to transform society. Mexicans seeking to destroy the power of the landholders or the Church, to bring "justice" to the urban or rural lower classes, to drive out the Yankee "imperialist," or merely to seize power for themselves—in short, virtually all groups to whom Marxism appealed in other parts of the world— could readily find a place in the ranks of one or another of the revolutionary chieftains. The national revolutionary process absorbed most of the attention and energies of the discontented in Mexico, leaving little room for the appeal of foreign ideologies. In any case, the few intellectuals and labor leaders who were attracted by foreign radical doctrines had greater affinity for anarchism than for Marxism.

It is significant that the Mexican Constitution of February 1917, an extremely radical document for the times, was prepared by men who knew little of Marxism. When the constituent assembly convened on November 21, 1916, nearly a year before the Russian Revolution, it included only one man who regarded himself as a Marxist. And this man, Luis G. Monzón, a school teacher from Sonora, was content at the time to follow the leadership of the revolutionary heroes Venustiano Carranza and Alvaro Obregón. He played no part in the subsequent establishment of the Mexican Communist Party.

Under the circumstances, for several years the Communist movement in Mexico was almost entirely the product of foreign organizers. The names of such non-Mexicans as the Americans Linn Gale, Charles Phillips, Luis Fraina, and Bertram D. Wolfe, the Russian Michael Borodin, the Indian Manabendra Nath Roy, the Japanese Sen Katayama, the Swiss Alfred Stirner, and the Cuban Julio Antonio Mella are still identified with the early years of the Communist party, but the names of most of the Mexican founders have been forgotten. Foreigners on the party's Executive Committee directed Communist activities in Mexico and usually spoke for the party at international Communist meetings during the 1920's.

The formal establishment of the Communist party in Mexico occurred in September 1919. It came about as a result of rivalry between the American radical Gale and the Indian nationalist Roy, both of whom tried unsuccessfully to take over the tiny Mexican Socialist party. Both men were accepted into that party, both were expelled, and each converted his faction into a "Communist party" seeking affiliation with the Communist International. In 1920 the party led by Roy was recognized by the Comintern. It has since remained the official Mexican Communist Party.

After the Second Congress of the Comintern in 1920 leadership of the party passed to Phillips, who was the dominant figure for about two years. He sent an enthusiastic report to the Comintern in 1922, indicating that the party then had fifteen hundred members. Katayama and Fraina were sent by the Comintern that same year to investigate and advise the Mexican party. They tried to root out anarchist tendencies among the membership and to persuade the Communists to participate actively in the national elections. Their influence was short-lived. Bertram Wolfe arrived in 1923. He was elected to the Executive Committee in 1924 and represented the Mexican party at the Comintern Congress held later that year. Wolfe reported that the party had one thousand members. One of his chief concerns was to make the party self-supporting and independent of Mexican government subsidies. His efforts in this direction were only temporarily successful. With Wolfe's departure in July 1925, American Communist influence over the Mexican party became less apparent, but other foreigners continued to play key roles in the Mexican Communist movement. For a time in 1927–1928, the Cuban exile Mella held influential posts in the party until he clashed with Stirner, a member of the Executive Committee, and with the Italian Communist Carlos Contreras,[1] a Comintern agent then acting as party adviser. It is evident that during the first decade Mexican Communists had few occasions to make important political decisions on their own. A rare exception occurred in 1929, when they decided to support the government during a revolt by disgruntled military leaders. This decision was bitterly criticized by the Comintern and led to another shake-up in party leadership.

For a short time after its founding it appeared that the Communist party might establish a significant foothold among the leaders of the Revolution. From the outset the party had a small peasant following and ranked demands for sweeping agrarian reform high on its program. Since agrarian reform was an integral part of the Mexican Revolution, several state governors and ambitious officials of the central government were willing to cooperate with the Communists. Adolfo de la Huerta, Secretary of Finance in the Obregón administration, courted the party before his abortive revolt in 1923, and such prominent revolutionary generals as Francisco Múgica, governor of Michoacán, and Felipe Carrillo Puerto, the "Socialist" governor of Yucatán, actually joined the party. These men and others were attracted by the political potential of the Communist organization rather than by its doctrines, of which they knew or understood almost nothing. Felipe Carrillo's abysmal ignorance of Marxism and its origins was revealed in his magnanimous offer to employ Marx and Engels on his staff if they should care to come to Yucatán.

---

1. This man has been known variously as Enea Sormenti, Arturo Sormenti, Carlos Contreras, and Vittorio Vidale. Under the latter, which is probably his true name, he served as top Communist party leader in Trieste after World War II. He used the alias Carlos Contreras in Mexico, Argentina, and Spain.

Without exception the well-known revolutionary figures drifted away from the Communist party as Obregón consolidated his position. Their close cooperation even for a brief time, however, had provided favorable circumstances in which the Communists were able to extend their influence among the rural populace. They penetrated existing agrarian "communes" and created new ones. The greatest advances were made in the state of Vera Cruz, where the Communists fielded several bands of peasant guerrillas against the de la Huerta forces during the 1923 rebellion. Their influence among the peasants remained significant until the 1930's, when peasant organizations were consolidated firmly under government control and reports of the enforced collectivization of the Russian peasantry destroyed any lingering illusions among Mexican officials that Soviet communism might be able to show them the way to agrarian reform.

As the revolutionary generals were leaving the Communist party another group of illustrious Mexicans entered it. These were the artists Diego Rivera, David Alfaro Siqueiros, Xavier Guerrero, and others whose paintings of the revolution had already begun to attract international attention. Imbued with zeal for international cooperation in art and culture, they were attracted by the international character of the Communist movement. They were no more doctrinaire Marxist-Leninists than the generals they replaced, but they played a far more important role in shaping the Communist party in Mexico. Rivera, Alfaro Siqueiros, and Guerrero were elected to the Executive Committee in 1923 and quickly came to dominate their lower-class compatriots in the party leadership. Their amateurish approach to politics was often a cause for concern to the Comintern, but they were long tolerated because their reputation as artists gave the party entree into high social and official circles that the proletarian labor and peasant leaders could not penetrate. Eventually, however, they were forced to give way to political leaders who enjoyed the full confidence of the international movement. Rivera was expelled from the party in the 1929 purge and became an ardent Trotskyist for several years, while Alfaro Siqueiros was removed, at least ostensibly, in 1940. Both men were later reinstated, and Alfaro Siqueiros was selected as head of the party in 1960. The identification of these men with the Communist movement over such a long period of time has given the Mexican party a stamp it still retains, even though the bulk of the leadership has been drawn from lower-class elements.

Uruguay

In nearly all important respects the environment and early experiences of the Communist party in Uruguay differed from those of the Mexican party. Socialism and the trade-union movement had taken root among the urban working class of Uruguay before the first world war. The country enjoyed political stability under representative government, and its citizens generally were more alert than Mexicans to events taking place outside the hemisphere. The Uruguayan Socialists followed closely and sympathetically news of the efforts by Russian "Socialists" to build a new kind of political order after 1917. Many of them identified themselves with the Russian experiment and felt that their party should affiliate with the Communist International when it was established in 1919. The debate over this issue was carried on within the Socialist Party of Uruguay for two years. At a Socialist party conclave in September–October 1920 three-quarters of the members were prepared to join the International, but the top leaders were unwilling to accept Lenin's "Twenty-one Conditions" for membership which had been set forth at the Second Comintern Congress in July of that year. The issue was settled at the party's annual convention in April 1921, when the overwhelming majority of the delegates, led by Eugenio Gómez, voted to adhere to the Comintern and to adopt the name Communist Party of Uruguay. The dissident minority withdrew to form a new Socialist party. The Communist party has since celebrated October 8, 1920 as its founding date.

The Communist Party of Uruguay had legal status from the outset, and throughout the 1920's enjoyed full freedom of operation. It failed, however, to attract a large following. Its membership was reported optimistically at 2,000 in 1922 and more realistically at 600 two years later. The party's efforts, like those of most other Uruguayan political groups, were confined largely to Montevideo and a few small towns. Yet, here, within a short time the Communists established an active press and a broad range of front groups that served as national affiliates of international Communist organizations. Building on a strong base in the maritime workers' union, the party competed with anarchists, syndicalists, and a revived Socialist party for control of the labor movement. These attempts met with only partial success, but by 1929 the Communists were able to set up a General Labor Confederation with a claimed membership of 14,000. It is significant that the party paid little attention to the rural populace, limiting its activities to presenting a presidential candidate on a "workers and peasants" ticket in the 1926 elections. He polled only 4,000 votes. In other electoral activities the party was more successful. It participated in each of the congressional contests, electing one congressman from Montevideo, Celestino Mibelli, in 1922 and adding another, Eugenio Gómez, in 1925. The party regularly elected a few candidates to the Montevideo Departmental Assembly. The Communist vote rose from twenty-nine hundred in 1922 to more than six thousand in 1931, a peak that was not to be equaled or surpassed for more than a decade.

The following and effectiveness of the Uruguayan party declined during the 1930's but reached its highest levels during the years of the second world war. Although the party retained formal legal standing, its activities were strictly curbed by the regime of authoritarian President Gabriel Terra, who held office from 1931 until 1938. Party leaders were jailed or exiled from time to time and the Communist press was frequently closed. Despite these restraints the Communists continued to participate in national politics, polling slightly over thirty-six hundred votes in 1934 and nearly fifty-eight hundred in 1938. Like their counterparts throughout Latin America, the Uruguayan Communists dutifully adopted the popular-front line in 1935, but their appeals for an alliance of "anti-Fascist" forces and the creation of a single national labor organization met with little response from other political groups. The party was further weakened by the Russo-German pact of 1939–1941. Although publicly the Communists denounced the "imperialist war" and continued to berate fascism, they pursued a policy of quiet cooperation with neo-Nazi groups during these years. The outbreak of war between Germany and the Soviet Union, however, brought an immediate reversal in the party's position and a dramatic rise in its popular following. Advocating complete subordination of partisan objectives to the war effort, the party polled nearly fifteen thousand votes in the 1942 elections, placing three Communists in the Chamber of Deputies. At the same time Communists cooperated with Socialists and others to form a single national labor confederation, which had fallen under full Communist control by 1945. At its peak in 1946 the Communist party included some fifteen thousand members and polled about thirty-three thousand votes to elect one senator and five congressmen.

Chile

The Communist movement was launched under more auspicious circumstances in Chile than in any other country of Latin America. The republic was ripe for social change. The first "people's president," Arturo Alessandri, had taken office just a year earlier, in December 1920, after a tempestuous campaign that had called national attention to the grievances of the common man and had raised popular expectations far beyond his capacity to satisfy them. The labor movement was large, well organized, politically alert, and highly self-conscious. Its major organization, the Chilean Workers' Federation with some 200,000 members, was controlled by men who were soon to become Communists, and who had already decided to affiliate it with the Communists' Red International of Labor Unions. The Chilean Communists, moreover, like their Uruguayan comrades, started with a party that was well established, with branches in most parts of the country, an effective electoral machine, and two representatives in the National Congress. This party, the Socialist Workers' Party of Chile, had been founded in 1912 by Luis Emilio Recabarren. In 1920 he had proposed that the party affiliate with the Comintern, but some of the other leaders were not yet willing to go so far. The proposal was repeated at the party's convention at Rancagua in December 1921 and was accepted unanimously. The formal adoption of the name Communist Party of Chile apparently took place on January 1, 1922. In all of Latin America the Chilean party was the only Socialist party that was transferred intact to the international Communist movement.

For five years the party was legal and highly active. It claimed two thousand members in 1922 and again two years later. The figure was probably inflated, but even though the party was not numerically strong there is no doubt that it was well financed and directed at this time. It maintained five separate daily newspapers as well as various weeklies and periodicals. In the elections of 1923 it returned two members to the Congress, while in 1926 two Communists were voted into the Senate and seven into the lower house.

The principal concern of the Communists in the early 1920's was to preserve their hold on organized labor against efforts by the government to register and take over the trade unions. They were successful through 1924, primarily because the Congress refused to support the president's program. In September of that year a military junta intervened to break the deadlock between the executive and the legislature, and Alessandri resigned. But in a complete turnabout a second military junta, led by Carlos Ibáñez, deposed the first one and recalled Alessandri in January 1925. During the next eight months most of Alessandri's reform program was put into effect and the Communist position in the labor movement began to erode. The party's political prestige, however, was still rising, as shown by the appointment of six Communists to the 100-member commission which drew up the Constitution of 1925. The head of the Communist delegation was Manuel Hidalgo, congressman and Secretary-General of the party after the suicide of Recabarren in 1924. The Alessandri regime fell in September 1925 after a clash between the President and his ambitious War Minister, Ibáñez. In the elections held later that year the Communists supported the only opposition candidate for the presidency. Although the candidate lost, he received a much larger protest vote than the

Communist party alone could deliver. Within a year the new President also clashed with Ibáñez and followed Alessandri into retirement. Almost immediately the regime cracked down on opposition elements, including the Communists. Hidalgo was deported; Elías Lafertte, Communist Secretary-General of the Chilean Workers' Federation, was sent to the remote island-prison colony of Mas Afuera; and other party leaders were jailed or exiled. Yet, the party participated in the 1927 presidential elections, again running the only opposition candidate. The Communist candidate, Lafertte, was still in prison and did not learn until later that he had competed for the presidency against strong man Ibáñez.

During Ibáñez' rule from 1927 to 1931 the position of the Communist party was largely destroyed. Its leadership was dispersed and almost as soon as new leaders were selected, they, too, were sent into exile. The party press was muzzled and the Communist-labor stronghold was taken over in large part by Socialists. By the end of the Ibáñez regime the Communist-controlled Chilean Workers' Federation had only about twenty-five thousand members. The party was also badly wracked by factionalism and became involved in a protracted dispute with the Comintern's South American Bureau. The most serious result was a split between the followers of Hidalgo and those of Lafertte. The schism persisted until 1937 when the Hidalgo group abandoned communism and merged with the Socialist party. The Lafertte faction retained the support of the Comintern and remained the official Communist Party of Chile.

In the political turbulence that followed the fall of Ibáñez the Communists demonstrated their complete inability to attract mass support either for party candidates at the polls or for a proletarian revolution. In the presidential elections of 1931 Lafertte was again a candidate, polling less than sixteen hundred votes. Hidalgo, representing the dissident faction, received a slightly larger total. The Communists sought in September to convert a spontaneous naval mutiny into a Soviet-style revolution and in December tried to set off a revolt within the army, but both efforts were quickly suppressed. The party refused to take part in the left-wing *coup d'état,* which established the short-lived Socialist Republic of Chile in June 1932, insisting that the new regime was a stalking horse for "imperialism." Their own hastily erected Revolutionary Council of Workers, Peasants, Soldiers, and Sailors attracted little attention. The collapse of the "Socialist Republic" brought new elections in October in which the official Communist party claimed that Lafertte had polled 4,652 votes for the presidency and that it had elected one senator and four congressmen. It actually placed one member in the Chamber of Deputies on a joint ticket. At the same time the dissident faction elected Hidalgo to the Senate and one member to the lower house, both on coalition slates. This poor showing of the Communist factions reflected the growing strength of the Chilean Socialist movement, which was largely unified in a new Socialist Party of Chile in 1933. Communist fortunes did not improve until the policy of open hostility toward the Socialist party was abandoned with the adoption of the popular-front line in 1935.

Brazil

Anarchism rather than socialism served as the springboard for the Communist movement in Brazil. During and immediately after World War I anarchist agitators penetrated the incipient labor movement, fomenting strikes and stimulating the formation of loosely organized trade unions and workers' associations. By 1918 they had attracted enough support to maintain a newspaper, *A Plebe.* In that same year in Pôrto Alegre they founded the small Maximalist Union, which included men who later became Communists. The Maximalist Union has been considered as the first Brazilian Communist organization. Anarchists were largely responsible for calling a national trade-union congress in 1920 to discuss the creation of a central labor body. But this congress, which failed in its purpose, marked the high point of anarchist influence in Brazil. Essentially an individualistic and negative philosophy, anarchism had been instrumental in arousing the aspirations of certain urban working-class groups without producing united leadership or a positive program for satisfying these aspirations. In the absence of a foreign political base to offset these deficiencies in direction and program, anarchism could not long compete with Soviet-inspired communism in Brazil.

Under the circumstances communism gradually replaced anarchism as the inspiration for the radical movement. An appreciable portion of the anarchists and other radicals in Brazil, like their counterparts elsewhere in Latin America, were attracted by the Soviet experiment in Russia. The works of Lenin and other Marxist writers were read by a growing number of leftist intellectuals and by some of the workers. The Maximalist Union in Pôrto Alegre established contact with Communist groups in Montevideo and Buenos Aires and received quantities of Soviet propaganda from these sources as well as directly from Moscow. Former anarchists such as Octavio Brandão, who gave public lectures on Russian culture to raise funds for the "victims of the White Terror," accepted communism and began forming small Communist groups in the larger cities and towns. On November 7, 1921, a Communist group with twelve members was founded in the national capital. This group took the initiative in organizing local Communist centers in the states of Rio de Janeiro, São Paulo, Minas Gerais, and later, Pernambuco. In January 1922 it launched a monthly publication, *Movimento Communista,* an avowed partisan of the Third International, to maintain contact and coordination between the scattered Communist nuclei.

The Communist Party of Brazil was formally organized at the First Party Congress, held in Rio de Janeiro and Niterói, March 25–27, 1922. A message of greetings from the Comintern was read to the delegates. The meeting was attended by delegates from Rio de Janeiro, Niterói, Cruzeiro, Recife, São Paulo, and Pôrto Alegre. Comparatively strong Communist groups in Santos and Juiz de Fora were not represented, but they quickly adhered to the new party. Although workers were included among the delegates, the Congress was dominated by intellectuals, as was the ten-member Executive Committee elected at that time. At least half the members of this Committee, moreover, represented the

Communist center in the national capital, which maintained its control over the fledgling party.

The founding of the Communist party was unheralded by the rest of Brazilan society, for the Communists were too few to attract notice. One of the party founders, Astrogildo Pereira, has stated that the combined membership of the seven Communist groups represented at the First Congress was only seventy-three persons out of a population of some thirty millions. The number of Communist sympathizers among intellectuals and within the ranks of urban labor greatly exceeded party membership, but it is probable that direct Communist influence did not extend to more than a few thousands in all Brazil. An indication of the strength of the Communist appeal among literate Brazilians is provided by circulation figures for the party publication, which averaged eighteen hundred copies per issue from January 1922 until it was suppressed in June 1923. Antonio Canelas, the party's representative to the Fourth Comintern Congress in December 1922, reported that there were then 500 Communists in Brazil. Two years later the report submitted by Astrogildo Pereira indicated a membership of only 350.

For about three months the Communist party operated openly, without interference by the authorities. In recent years Communist leaders have implied that the party was founded clandestinely and that from the outset it was vigorously opposed by a frightened, reactionary government. This view, however, greatly exaggerates the importance of the Communist party in Brazil in the 1920's. During most of that decade the chronic unrest that contributed to the growth of the Communist movement was expressed more directly in a series of politico-military uprisings in widely scattered parts of the country. In July 1922, in the wake of a short-lived revolt within the armed forces, the government decreed a state of siege and intensified police action against subversive elements. The decree was not directed specifically against the Communists, but it had the incidental effect of driving the party underground. For the next twenty-three years the Communist party was illegal, although the degree of illegality varied from time to time and from place to place according to the diligence and political views of local authorities.

The Communists adjusted quickly to their new status. As former anarchists, many of the members were accustomed to operating outside the law, and in any event they sought to avoid violence and overt political activity until they could build a more extensive party organization. They concentrated their attentions heavily, but not exclusively, on penetration of the urban labor movement. In 1923 the party reached an accommodation with the government-approved Brazilian Cooperative Syndicalist Confederation, which permitted the Communists to use the Confederation as a legal front for their activities. For more than a year this arrangement provided them a full page in the pro-administration daily newspaper, *O Paiz*—space which they used to full advantage. It seems likely that the arrangement between the Confederation and the Communists had the blessings of the Bernardes administration, perhaps as a gambit to win labor support for the government. If this was the case, however, the government's tactics failed, for the soft policy toward the Communist party produced no noticeable quickening of labor sympathy for the regime. The arrangement was broken off in 1924, but not until after the Communists had established cells in the leading trade unions, particularly those in small industries and in the transportation sector.

In 1925 the Brazilian Communists held their Second Congress. The leadership reported with satisfaction on the progress that had been made. Additional intellectuals had been drawn into the party and specialized youth and women's organizations had been established. The party was now organized under a national plan, with branches in all major cities. Its structure was consciously patterned after the Soviet example to give the Central Committee close control over all components. New officers were chosen, and it was probably at this time that Astrogildo Pereira was elected as the first Secretary-General of the Brazilian party.

An important decision of the Second Congress, and one indicative of the Communists' capabilities at that time, was to publish a weekly newspaper, *A Classe Operaria,* which appeared more or less regularly for about four years. It was printed by one of the leading dailies in Rio de Janeiro, and the bulk of each issue was sold directly, through party cells, in factories and in working-class neighborhoods. It began with a circulation of about nine thousand copies and reached a peak of about thirty thousand before it was finally closed in 1929.

Several factors contributed to the growth of the Communist organization and its influence during the mid-1920's. In the first place, the true nature of the party and its potential strength were not understood by the government, which was preoccupied with immediate problems of rebellion and political turmoil. In any event the Communist party was considered too small to pose a serious threat to the central authority. Nominally, the party was kept under police surveillance, but except for occasional harassment, such as the temporary closure of its press, it was allowed to operate with a minimum of interference. In some areas, moreover, only Communists within the foreign population seem to have been affected. Communist strength was equated in terms of labor agitation by the foreign colony in São Paulo, for example, where the police felt they were keeping communism under control by periodically deporting the most-active foreign agitators. The attitude of the police reflected the popular opinion that communism was confined primarily to the non-Brazilian population. While there is no question that Spanish and Italian immigrants were active in the labor movement in such industrial centers as São Paulo and Rio de Janeiro, there is no evidence that foreign nationals predominated in the Communist party in any area of Brazil.

After 1925 Communist efforts in the labor movement began to bear fruit. The number of party cells in various industrial and transportation enterprises increased greatly, and special attention was given to penetration of sailors' and dock workers' organizations. Santos, the principal port of Brazil, became a Communist bastion. In 1927 the Communists collaborated with anarchists to form a Workers' Federation of Rio de Janeiro, which they came to dominate. At about the same time, the Workers' Federation of São Paulo, the last anarchist stronghold in Brazil, fell under Communist control. The Communists were also in-

fluential in the so-called General Workers' Union, a loose
federation of trade unions in the Northeast. By 1929 the party
was able to set up a national labor body, the General Labor
Confederation of Brazil, which claimed about sixty thousand
members. While this was largely a paper organization, it served
as a vehicle for spreading Communist influence within the labor
movement.

The Brazilian party was somewhat slower than its contemporaries in Spanish America to engage in national politics. Although it had presented candidates for public office at the
municipal level in Santos as early as 1925, another two years
elapsed before the Communists were willing or able to compete
in elections at the national level. In line with Soviet directives
the Brazilian party in 1927 was instrumental in organizing a
Worker-Peasant Bloc, comprised chiefly of urban middle-class
groups, which served as a front for its electoral activities. In that
year the Bloc presented two candidates for Congress, a noncommunist, who was elected, and a Communist, who was not. Octavio
Brandão and another candidate on the Worker-Peasant ticket
were elected in 1928 to the municipal assembly of Rio de Janeiro. In 1929 the Communists, through the Worker-Peasant
Bloc, endorsed an impressive list of candidates to vie for national,
state, and local office in the national elections the following
year. Not a single one was elected.

The failure at the polls resulted from a series of crises that
wracked the Communist party in 1929. At its Third Congress,
held in late December and early January of 1928–1929, there had
been strong indications of dissatisfaction with the Worker-Peasant Bloc. A vociferous faction, including some persons prominent in the party leadership, had protested that the party would
be submerged and lose its distinctive proletarian identity by
involving itself in a peasant–middle-class movement. As former
anarchists, these members had little concern for the peasants and
regarded all so-called bourgeois elements as the enemies of the
true proletariat, which in their view was limited to the urban
working class. At the same time the Comintern had called for
a rigidly independent Communist position in the labor move-

ment, prohibiting further cooperation with noncommunist groups. This line provoked bitter opposition by some of the party's labor leaders, who were expelled at the Third Congress. The Communist party's position in the labor movement was also adversely affected by the Stalin-Trotsky feud, which was then rocking the international Communist organization. A significant portion of the remaining Communist labor leaders and some of the top youth leaders of the party withdrew in 1929 to form a Trotskyist organization, which for a time appears to have had a larger following than the official Communist party. In addition to these internal difficulties, the Communists were also faced with increasing hostility by the regime. A series of strikes in 1929 involving both dissident and disciplined Communists led the government to crack down on labor activities generally and on the Communist party in particular. Most of the party's overt apparatus was destroyed and such influence as it had retained was badly undermined.

The ideological and tactical differences that divided the Brazilian Communists were further crystallized by the revolution of 1930. After a brief uprising in October of that year, Getulio Vargas was swept into power at the head of a heterogeneous alliance that included most of the political and military figures who had been advocating social and political reforms since 1922. In view of Vargas' appeal to the masses, many Communists had enlisted under his banner and attempted to persuade the party to align itself formally with his Liberal Alliance. This the party refused to do. In conformity with the Comintern line at that period, Communist leaders denounced Vargas and continued to call vainly for a strictly proletarian revolution under their direction. They were particularly vehement in attacking the views of Luiz Carlos Prestes, one of the few rebels of the 1920's who refused to support Vargas but insisted that the Communist party should join forces with other discontented groups in an attempt to seize power. All Communists who followed Vargas or Prestes were expelled from the party, leaving its already decimated ranks slightly, if any, larger than they had been in 1922. The Communists were thus completely isolated from the main currents of

Brazilian political thought and action, and were to remain so until a change in the Comintern line permitted them to endorse Prestes' views and accept his leadership in 1935.

In the mid-1930's, while Communists elsewhere in Latin America were switching to the popular-front strategy, the Brazilian party was planning a leftist revolution under Communist direction. The abortive revolt of 1935 left the party decimated for nearly ten years.[2]

The amnesty of Communist leaders and the restoration of legal status to the party in April 1945 gave the Brazilian Communists the first real opportunity to test their appeal and organizational ability in an open political climate. Their success surprised noncommunists generally and was a source of considerable concern to the Dutra administration. Within two years, as its membership soared from some 4,000 to about 150,000, the party became clearly the largest Communist organization in the Western Hemisphere. Exploiting to the maximum the great personal popularity of Luiz Carlos Prestes and the widespread fervor for democratic reforms following the overthrow of the fifteen-year Vargas regime, the Communists ran fourth among all Brazilian parties in the national elections of December 1945. Their unknown presidential candidate polled nearly 570,000 votes—close to 10 per cent of the total—while well over half a million votes were cast for Communist candidates to the Constituent Assembly. Prestes was elected to the Senate and fourteen Communists were elected to the Chamber of Deputies. The Communist vote was larger than the combined total for seven of the twelve parties competing in the elections. Thirteen months later, in the supplemental elections for Congress and for state offices, the party retained its fourth rank, placing two candidates in Congress, forty-six in fifteen state legislatures, and a plurality of eighteen in the municipal assembly of the federal district. The party had shown that it could attract nearly one-tenth of the electorate throughout the country and it was still growing.

The success of the Brazilian party was due largely to its moderation and to the favorable international situation. When

---

2. See Chapter 7.

both of these factors changed its fortunes declined rapidly. In their propaganda the Communists sought to deny their revolutionary heritage and to exploit lingering wartime illusions about the "democratic" Soviet Union, with whom they were openly identified. Their domestic program called for moderate reforms which threatened no violence to Brazilian institutions. With the beginning of the cold war, however, the party's rapid growth and its identification with the Soviet Union proved to be liabilities. The Brazilian government, moreover, could not be certain of the loyalty of the Communists, particularly in view of Prestes' statement, repeated on various occasions after March 1946, that in the event of war between Brazil and the Soviet Union the Communists would take up arms against Brazil. Although this statement was not then widely believed, it was used as partial justification for outlawing the party in May 1947 and for canceling the mandates of Communists in public office the following January. With the loss of legal status and the right to run its candidates openly, the Communist party quickly ceased to be a major political force.

THE SECOND WAVE

While the five original Communist parties were building on Socialist or Anarchist foundations during the 1920's, entirely new Communist and Communist-oriented groups were emerging in a majority of the other Latin American republics. In each case the Communist organizations in the second wave had to contend with more serious obstacles than their predecessors had initially faced. These handicaps included the almost complete absence of labor organizations, little or no tradition of radical political movements, and suppression of opposition groups by regimes that were either highly authoritarian or outright dictatorships.

An indication of the growth of the Communist movement in the middle and late 1920's was given in two regional congresses held by the Latin American Communists in 1929. In May of that year a Communist labor congress at Montevideo was attended by delegates and observers from fifteen Latin American countries, and all but one of these countries were represented at a Communist political gathering in Buenos Aires the following month. These countries were: Argentina, Bolivia, Brazil, Colombia, Cuba, Ecuador, El Salvador, Guatemala, Mexico, Panama, Paraguay, Peru, Uruguay, and Venezuela. The Chilean Communists, who certainly qualified for attendance at both meetings, were unable to be present. Costa Rica, which had no Communist party at that date, sent an observer only to the Montevideo Congress, and the small Communist group in Honduras was apparently not represented by its own delegates at either meeting.

The strength of the Communist movement was not as great as it appeared in mid-1929, for there were only eight avowed Communist parties in all of Latin America at that time. There was not even the shadow of a Communist or Communist-front party in Venezuela in 1929, and Bolivia was not to have a formal Communist political organization for twenty years. Nevertheless, it was evident that less than twelve years after the Russian Revolution the Communist movement had outlets or active spokesmen in all but three countries of Latin America. It was probably only coincidence that two of these three countries were then occupied by United States Marines and the third had been occupied for eight of the preceding fifteen years.

Guatemala

The earliest of the new Communist groups appears to have been the Socialist Labor Unification, formed in Guatemala some time after the overthrow of dictator Estrada Cabrera in 1920. The leaders of this group requested the Mexican party in 1923 to assist them in converting their organization into a Communist party. The conversion was apparently completed in 1924, the year in which the Guatemalan party was recognized by the Comintern. At that time it was thought that the party in Guatemala might serve as a nucleus for a Communist Party of Central America. This premise underlay the cooperation between Communist agents from Guatemala and Mexico, who in 1925 organized the first Communist group in El Salvador.

El Salvador

The Salvadoran party has since dated its origin from that year, but it appears to have operated entirely behind the façade of the labor movement and international Communist-front organizations for several years. By 1930, or perhaps even earlier, however, the regional-party concept had been abandoned and the Salvadoran Communists were issuing proclamations and carnets in the name of the Communist Party of El Salvador.

Cuba

An avowed Communist party was established in Cuba in 1925 and was admitted to the Comintern in 1928. The first formal Communist organization in Cuba, the Communist Group of Havana, had been legally constituted in 1923, while informal Marxist study groups had sprung up in other parts of the island at about the same time. By early 1925 the various Communist groups were suppressed by the Machado regime, which was rapidly becoming a dictatorship. Persecution had the unanticipated effect of driving the scattered Communists together. On August 16, 1925, Marxist labor groups led by Carlos Baliño merged with groups of self-styled Communists among Cuban university students to form the Communist Party of Cuba. The students were led by Julio Antonio Mella, who became the first Secretary-General of the party. The Cuban party was almost immediately outlawed by the Machado government and its leaders imprisoned. Baliño died while awaiting trial and Mella was exiled. He was assassinated in Mexico in 1929, allegedly by an agent of Machado. The loss of these leaders and the continued repressive measures of the dictatorship impeded the growth of the Communist movement in Cuba but did not prevent the Communists from infiltrating the National Labor Confederation and becoming one of the more influential revolutionary organizations in the country.

There was little in the early experience of the Cuban Communists to suggest that they would be the first in Latin America to enter an effective alliance with the government and to build a truly mass party. They achieved this result by throwing their support to the dictator in exchange for legal status and a free hand in the labor movement. Their first such effort, in the waning days of the Machado regime, failed miserably. The party was isolated from the noncommunist revolutionaries who took office in August 1933 and comprised the principal opposition to Cuban strong man Fulgencio Batista after January 1934. Unable to reach an accommodation with the opposition during the popular-front period, the Communists turned to Batista, who permitted them gradually to increase their activities. A portion of the Communists, led by Juan Marinello, joined with Socialists and dissidents from the larger parties to establish the Revolutionary Union Party in 1937. The Communist press was published openly after May 1938. Following an interview between Secretary-General Blas Roca and Batista, the main Communist group was granted legal status as the Communist Party of Cuba in September 1938 and the Communist Lázaro Peña became the first head of the Cuban Labor Confederation, founded in January 1939. Eight months later the two Communist parties merged to form the Communist Revolutionary Union, which helped to elect Batista to the presidency in 1940 and remained part of the government coalition throughout his administration.

The alliance with Batista was highly successful for the Communists. Their privileged position as valued supporters of the regime permitted them to escape the setbacks suffered by most other Latin American Communist parties at the time of the unexpected Hitler-Stalin pact in 1939. Rather, party membership and electoral following increased rapidly once they had gained legal recognition and leadership of organized labor. Six Communists were included among the seventy-six members of the Constituent Assembly which drafted the Constitution of 1940, and in the congressional elections of that year the party polled over eighty thousand votes to win eight seats in the Chamber of Deputies. The political importance and respectability of the Communists were revealed with the appointment of Juan Marinello as Minister without Portfolio in Batista's cabinet in March 1943. When Marinello resigned to run for the Senate in the June 1944 elections, his cabinet post was taken by another Communist intellectual, Carlos Rafael Rodríguez. These were the first Communists to hold such high positions in any Latin American government. The party, known as the Popular Socialist Party after January 1944, increased its vote by 50 per cent in the June elections even though the administration candidate for the presidency was defeated. Over 120,000 votes were cast for Communist candidates to elect three senators and seven deputies. Emerging as one of the leading political forces in Cuba, the Communists were able to enter the administration bloc under new President Grau San Martín, who gave them half the top labor posts and the vice-presidency of the Senate in exchange for their congressional support. The party's prestige remained high and the number of registered Communist voters continued to mount until it reached a high approaching 160,000 in the late 1940's. The arrangement with President Grau was terminated in 1947, and under the Prío administration after 1948 Communist political and labor power was seriously reduced. Without these bases the Communist organization quickly crumbled. The party was again a minor political organization when outlawed by the second Batista regime in 1953. Nevertheless, for a full decade—longer than any other Latin American Communist party—it had enjoyed the benefits of close association with the government. The experience acquired by Communist leaders during that period was to prove an invaluable asset to the party after 1959.

Paraguay

The Paraguayan Communist Party was founded in 1928 and admitted into the Comintern later that same year. The new party consisted of a few former anarchists active in the tiny labor movement in Asunción and a small group of young intellectuals who had already begun to regard themselves as Communists. One of these, Obdulio Barthe, is still prominent in the leadership of the party. It began its existence as a clandestine organization and has been proscribed almost continuously since. A delegate to the Communist conference in Buenos Aires in 1929 described the party at that time as "a handful of urban workers." During the next few years it grew slowly if at all. In 1932 the international Communist press reported that "it consists of one little group only which has only a very limited influence on the trade unions." Subsequently the party was able to expand its operations and membership substantially during brief respites between dictatorships in the mid-1930's and the mid-1940's. On the latter occasion it claimed 8,000 members. In both instances, however, Communist gains were quickly reversed as the country returned to authoritarian rule. Even at its height the Paraguayan party has never been an important element in national politics.

* * *

In four Latin American countries in the 1920's, the men who became Communists first operated within other parties. In Colombia and Ecuador, left-wing groups, including some individuals who even then advocated adherence to the Comintern, formed Socialist parties in 1926. Even though a majority of the leaders rejected suggestions that their parties adopt the Communist name, the Socialist Revolutionary Party of Colombia and the Ecuadoran Socialist Party were accepted by the Comintern with one-half vote each in 1928. Those who later formed the Communist party in Peru were initially attracted to the APRA movement, founded by Haya de la Torre in 1924. When it was evident that APRA would not become part of the international apparatus directed by the Soviet Union, these men broke away to establish the Peruvian Socialist Party in 1928. This small organization was led by José Carlos Mariátegui, the only important Marxist theoretician to arise in Latin America. Although Mariátegui seemed basically in sympathy with international communism, he differed with the Comintern on certain points of ideology and strategy and did not seek to affiliate his party with the international movement. Subsequently, both Socialists and Communists in Peru have claimed him as their guiding spirit, although he died before deciding whether to accept or reject Comintern discipline. The Panamanian Communists comprised only a small segment within the insignificant *Laborista* party, which could attract only about one-fortieth of the vote cast in national elections.

Honduras

Perhaps the most nebulous Communist organization in Latin America in the 1920's existed in Honduras. It had been organized in the middle or later years of the decade by Juan Pablo Wainwright, a Honduran adventurer who also figured in the Communist movement in Guatemala and El Salvador. Since the Central American Communists at that time were to be grouped into a single party, the Honduran Communists did not initially create a political apparatus separate from their cells in the national labor federation. They seem to have remained content with only a labor front for some time after the regional-party concept had been dropped and after they had set up their own Honduran Syndical Federation in 1929. By January 1932 the party had emerged sufficiently to publish a monthly bulletin in its own name. In that same month, however, the Honduran labor movement and the Communist party were obliterated by the Carías regime.

THIRD-PERIOD PARTIES

At its Sixth Congress in 1928 the Comintern adopted the line that Soviet historians have since identified with the so-called "third period" of the Communist International. This line called for Communists everywhere to declare themselves as such, to cease cooperation with "bourgeois" and "leftist reformist" elements, and to establish purely Communist organizations which should strive to foment and seize the leadership of proletarian revolutions. Repercussions were felt in every phase of Communist activities in Latin America. With respect to their political apparatus, the Comintern directives made it clear that in countries where Communists operated within other parties every effort should be made to convert these parties into full-fledged Communist organizations. In conformity with these directives, a majority of the leaders of the Peruvian Socialist Party in 1930 voted to adopt the name Peruvian Communist Party and to seek affiliation with the Comintern. In Colombia most of the non-communist directors of the Socialist Revolutionary Party had abandoned it before the 1930 elections, thus permitting the remaining leaders to convert it into the Communist Party of Colombia at a special convention held on July 17, 1930. In that same year the Panamanian Communists withdrew from the *Laborista* party to form the Communist Party of Panama. The process of transforming the Ecuadoran Socialist Party into a strictly Communist organization required about two years, during which those factions unwilling to submit to the Comintern were sloughed off. Formal adoption of the name Communist Party of Ecuador was approved in 1931.

Ecuador

The party in Ecuador is unique in Latin America in being the only one that has ever had a member, even briefly, in the national executive, and it is one of three that has been represented in the national cabinet. After years of marginal existence, during which it slowly extended its influence among intellectuals and in the student and labor movements in Quito and Guayaquil, the Communist party joined with Socialists and Liberals in the successful revolt which brought President Velasco Ibarra to power in May 1944. One Communist, Gustavo Becerra, was included in the provisional junta which exercised executive power for three days until Velasco's return from exile. In the Constituent Assembly elections of July 23 the Communist party won fifteen of the eighty-nine seats, and Communist poet Pedro Vera was selected as Secretary when the Assembly convened on August 10. Later that month Velasco appointed Communist Alfredo Vera y Vera to his cabinet as Minister of Public Instruction. Minister Vera served for five months, being dismissed in January 1945 when Velasco broke with his left-wing supporters. Out of office, the Communist party quickly declined in membership and political significance.

Costa Rica

The Communist Party of Costa Rica was established in 1929 by a young intellectual, Manuel Mora, who still heads the Communist movement in his country. The party was founded openly and retained freedom of operation during the Depression years, when Communists in most of Latin America were driven underground. Somewhat less vehement than other Communist organizations in calling for Soviet-style revolution, it gained respect as the only Costa Rican party at that time concerned for the welfare of the lower classes. The character of the party in its early years was influenced by Rómulo Betancourt, then a political exile from his native Venezuela. Betancourt recalls that he was attracted to communism by his belief that Soviet Russia was forging a "social organization of world-wide validity." He soon came to question the universality of Marxist-Leninist doctrine as interpreted by Soviet Communists, however, and to advocate that the Latin American parties develop independently, without subservience to the Comintern. The Costa Rican party was not accepted as a full member of the Comintern until 1935, after Betancourt had broken away to form an indigenous social-revolutionary movement for Venezuela.

Haiti

Two intellectuals, Max Hudicourt and Jacques Roumain, created the ephemeral Communist Party of Haiti during a brief period of open political activity in mid-1930. They attracted only a few followers, primarily in Port-au-Prince, and were unable to exert any influence on the elections held that year. The Vincent regime which took office in November 1930, exiled the two leaders. Hudicourt sought refuge in the United States while Roumain went to Mexico, where he was serving as his country's diplomatic representative at the time of his death in 1944. The small Communist organization, moribund after the expulsion of Hudicourt and Roumain, was formally proscribed in 1936. The Haitian party completely disappeared for the next decade.

Venezuela

The first organized Communist activity by Venezuelans was carried on outside the country by exiles from the Juan Vicente Gómez dictatorship who had joined Communist parties elsewhere during the 1920's. At least one of these, Aurelio Fortoul Briceño, was associated with the Caribbean Bureau of the Comintern in New York. The exiles organized a Communist-front Venezuelan Revolutionary Party in New York in 1926, and a provisional Central Committee for a Communist Party of Venezuela, probably in Colombia, in 1930. Meanwhile, clandestine Communist "study circles" sprang up among students within Venezuela between 1928 and 1930, but these were uncoordinated and usually short-lived. Fortoul slipped into Caracas in January 1931 and began the task or organizing a regular party. The first cell was created on March 5, 1931, the date now generally accepted for the formal founding of the party. A month later there were six cells with a total of twenty-seven members, including both students and workers, meeting regularly in Caracas, and organizational activity had been extended to neighboring cities. In late May, however, Fortoul and nine other organizers were arrested, and the infant party was severely repressed. It survived, but was unable to grow significantly until after the death of Gómez in December 1935. Earlier that year the Venezuelan party was granted full membership in the Comintern.

The Venezuelan party maintained a continuous existence after 1931, despite the serious handicaps of external repression and internal factionalism. Until the end of World War II, however, it was frequently overshadowed by front parties, apparently democratic organizations in which Communists worked closely with members of the noncommunist Left. The more important of these short-lived political vehicles were: the Venezuelan Organization Movement, 1936; the National Democratic Party, 1936–1938; and the Venezuelan Popular Union, 1943–1946.

With the overthrow of the Medina regime in 1945 the Communist party gained legal status, but almost immediately fragmented. For several years it was not possible to determine which of several competing Communist groups was the authentic Communist party, although there was always at least one Communist Party of Venezuela. The outstanding dissident faction—and the only rival organization acceptable to international Communist authorities—was the Revolutionary Party of the Communist Proletariat. It split off from the Communist Party of Venezuela in 1947 and survived until 1952, when most of its members rejoined the parent body.

THE FOURTH WAVE

The fourth wave of Communist organizational activity in Latin America, from the mid-1930's to the mid-1940's, can be subdivided into three periods, each corresponding to a distinct episode in the annals of the international Communist movement. These were the periods of the Popular Front, which had begun in Latin America by 1935, the Hitler-Stalin pact, from August 1939 to June 1941, and the remaining years of the second world war. A new party was established in Latin America during each of these episodes.

Nicaragua

The period of the Popular Front witnessed the emergence of the only Communist party in Latin America that has never called itself Communist. This is the Socialist Party of Nicaragua, created in 1937 by a minority bloc which broke away from the Workers' party to oppose the election of Anastasio Somoza. The Communists operated openly for about two years, until their activities were banned under the 1939 Constitution. At that time the party was suppressed and most of its leaders driven into exile. During World War II, however, the Communists cooperated with the Somoza regime and were permitted to assume a leading position in the new labor confederation. Despite the legal ban against "parties organized on an international basis," the Communists took part in the national elections of 1947. But within a year both the party and the labor confederation were dissolved by the government, and since that time the Nicaraguan Communists have been forced to operate entirely underground.

Bolivia

Less than six months after the signing of the Hitler-Stalin pact, a leftist party was formed in Bolivia. This organization, the Party of the Revolutionary Left, was not a Communist party in the usual sense. In fact, in terms of Marxist-Leninist doctrine it left a great deal to be desired, and its leaders then stoutly denied that it was Communist. It seems fitting that this party should emerge during the brief honeymoon between Communists and Nazis, when ideological distinctions between them were deliberately blurred, for the Bolivian radicals had been slow to make clear distinctions among the many conflicting doctrines then current. Prior to 1940 only the Trotskyists had precipitated out of the nebulous Bolivian radical movement. The Party of the Revolutionary Left was important because it provided the first political organization in which others who regarded themselves as Communists could work together at the national level. While it did not maintain close ties with international communism, it served in effect as the Communist political apparatus in the republic until a large part of its membership broke away to establish the formal Communist Party of Bolivia in 1949.

Dominican Republic

The Communist party in the Dominican Republic owes its existence indirectly to the civil war in Spain. Of the thousands of loyalist refugees from that conflict, some nine hundred found haven in the Dominican Republic after 1939. Over one hundred of these, Spaniards and Catalans, were Communists, who set up their own front organizations and were soon providing inspiration and example to local citizens. The exile groups were particularly active among students at the national university, some of whom had already become Communists in other Latin American countries. The student nucleus established a separate Dominican Communist Party in 1942. Although the party was illegal, it was tolerated until 1945, when most of its leaders were deported. The following year, however, when dictator Rafael Trujillo was eager to demonstrate that democracy flourished in his realm, the

Communists were invited to return and to establish a legal party. Their organization then took the name Popular Socialist Party, which it still retains. The Communists ran candidates in the national elections but did not win any public offices. In 1947, when it could be of no further use to him, Trujillo outlawed the party and again banished its leaders. The Popular Socialist Party became strictly an exile organization. There was no more Communist activity within the Dominican Republic until after the assassination of Trujillo in May 1961.

The action of the Dominican Communists in changing the name of their party was not at all unique at that time. The Communist party in Nicaragua had been known as the Socialist Party since 1937, and two years later the Cuban organization took the name Communist Revolutionary Union. There was a rash of name changing after the Comintern was formally dissolved in May 1943. Within a year, four Latin American Communist parties dropped the Communist label in attempts to prove their independence from Moscow. Thus, the Costa Rican party became the Popular Vanguard and the Panamanian Communists called their organization the Party of the People. The Colombian party was registered in 1944 as the Social Democratic Party, but reverted to Communist Party of Colombia in 1947. The most fashionable of the new names was Popular Socialist Party, which the Cuban Communists adopted in January 1944. After the war, in 1946, this name was used not only by the Dominicans, but also by some of the Communists in Haiti.

POSTWAR COMMUNIST PARTIES

By the end of World War II, a Communist party organization had been formed in each of the twenty Latin American republics. Several of these were moribund, however, and at least one did not yet enjoy full standing in the international Communist community. Therefore, in the postwar years Communist organizational activities have been directed toward reincarnating long-defunct parties and enhancing the efficiency of others rather than toward the systematic creation of new national Communist parties, as in earlier periods. Since 1946 the Communists have generally followed a pragmatic approach, displaying considerable flexibility in allowing local conditions and changes in the international situation to influence their organizational policy in various countries of Latin America.

Haiti

The temporary revival of communism in Haiti was complicated by the emergence of two rival Communist parties shortly after the overthrow of the Lescot regime in January 1946. The first of these pre-empted the name Communist Party of Haiti. It was founded by a Haitian Protestant cleric, Félix d'Orleans Juste Constant, a radical who appears to have been more maverick than Marxist. Constant issued a revolutionary program designed to appeal to the masses, but he called also for close, effective cooperation with the United States. The other party, which took the Popular Socialist label, was a reincarnation of the Communist party established in 1930. One of the founders of the early party, Max Hudicourt, returned from exile in the United States to lead the new organization. It was soon echoing the approved international Communist line. In the national elections of 1946 Hudicourt was elected to the Senate and another Popular Socialist candidate, Rossini Pierre-Louis, won a seat in the Chamber of Deputies. Constant's party failed to elect a candidate to national office. It was outlawed in February 1948, at which time Constant announced that it had voluntarily dissolved the preceding April. Hudicourt was assassinated in 1947, and without his leadership the Popular Socialist Party rapidly deteriorated. It survived as an ineffectual organization until November 1949, when it, too, was outlawed. Neither party had managed to attract a significant following, with the result that the rigorous suppression of Communist activity under the Magloire regime (1950–1956) destroyed the Communist movement in Haiti for the second time in a single generation.

Mexico

The effort to revive the communist movement took a different turn in Mexico, where an unusual situation existed. There the formal Communist party enjoyed legal status but fell far short of the membership required for full participation in national elections. In addition, a splinter group, the Mexican Worker-Peasant Party, which had broken away from the Communist party in 1940, also operated legally but ineffectually on the national scene. No effort was made to merge these two or to strengthen either of them. Instead, a new, procommunist party was added. In 1947 the large People's Party was established by Vicente Lombardo Toledano, head of the Communist-front Latin American Labor Confederation. It was not an orthodox-Communist organization, although it was avowedly Marxist and, in fact, Marxist-Leninist in orientation. There is no clear evidence to show whether the founding of the People's Party was fortuitous or in response to international Communist directives. The complete absence of the vituperative attacks usually heaped on heretical Marxist organizations by the international movement, however, suggests that the party was established with Moscow's blessing. The People's Party regularly differed with the Communist party over domestic political tactics, for Lombardo was more willing than the Communists to cooperate with the regime. But all differences between them disappeared in their treatment of international issues. The People's Party has followed every twist and turn in the international Communist line, supporting all of the Soviet-inspired propaganda campaigns endorsed by the regular Communist parties of Latin America. In October 1960 the party added the word "Socialist" to its name, and in 1963 absorbed the tiny Mexican Worker-Peasant Party, but otherwise has made no meaningful change in organization or orientation since its founding. It is still not regarded as a formal part of the international Communist political apparatus, but it carries most of the propaganda burden that the small Mexican Communist Party is incapable of supporting.

Guatemala

The most spectacular resurgence of a moribund Communist movement occurred in Guatemala in the postwar decade. The party had almost completely disintegrated under the Ubico dictatorship after 1930, with its few leaders either jailed or exiled. With the revolutions of 1944, which overthrew the dictator and gave Guatemala a truly open political climate for the first time, the exiles began filtering back into the country. Several of them had been active in other Communist parties, where they had acquired organizational skills in woefully short supply among the new and inexperienced political groups then forming in Guatemala. The Communists, however, did not move quickly to reestablish the party. Rather, they infiltrated noncommunist revolutionary parties and concentrated on building strength in the newly organized labor movement. Not until September 1947 did a Communist group within the Revolutionary Action Party form a clandestine organization known as the Democratic Vanguard. Two years later, after failing to convert the Revolutionary Action Party into a Communist party, the Democratic Vanguard withdrew to become the Communist Party of Guatemala. It did not emerge into the open until 1950. A parallel communist organization, known as the Revolutionary Workers' Party of Guatemala, was established openly in mid-1950. The two merged, on orders from Moscow, late in 1951. The united Communist party changed its name to Guatemalan Labor Party and was granted legal status in December 1952. By this time Communists held commanding positions in the labor movement, in the educational system, in some peasant organizations, and in some of the noncommunist parties. Many of these organizations had been grouped into a National Democratic Front to support the presidential campaign of Jacobo Arbenz. After Arbenz' election, the Communist and procommunist leaders of the National Democratic Front served as an informal advisory board on national policies.

Thus, for eighteen months after gaining legal status the Communist party was in fact the strongest political organization in Guatemala. But, even though it was close to power, it lacked strong support among the people. This was illustrated clearly by the collapse of the communist apparatus when the Arbenz regime was overthrown in mid-1954. None of the workers and peasants, for whom the party had presumed to speak, rose to its defense when Castillo Armas' makeshift invasion army entered the country.

Bolivia

About the time that the Communist party was being organized in Guatemala, a formal Communist party was founded in Bolivia by Communists who had split off from the Party of the Revolutionary Left. It was the first such organization in Bolivia to gain full recognition from the international Communist movement. An earlier, self-styled Communist party did not receive international sanction and was unable to survive the death of its leader in 1946. The new Communist Party of Bolivia was an illegal, underground party from 1949 until 1952, when the noncommunist National Revolutionary Movement seized power by revolution. The party still enjoys all of the benefits of legal standing, but has been unable to exert strong appeal on either urban or rural masses, and plays no significant part in national affairs.

Honduras

In its present manifestation, the Communist Party of Honduras is the youngest Communist political organization on the mainland of Latin America. The original party apparatus was shattered in 1932 and could not resume operations during the long dictatorship of President Tiburcio Carías. A faint stirring of leftist activity in 1946 was sufficient to provoke the government to issue an anticommunist decree which is still in effect. Following the revolution of 1948, political controls were relaxed and several new parties developed. Among these was the leftist Democratic Revolutionary Party of Honduras, which the Communists penetrated and came to dominate. They used this vehicle until 1953, when it was driven underground and its leaders fled to Guatemala. A handful of Communists managed to remain active among banana workers on the northern coast and in the small organized labor movement in Tegucigalpa, but they attracted few followers. For five years they appear to have had no formal party organization. Finally, in May 1958, a group of labor leaders and students in Tegucigalpa organized the Communist party in its present form. It obtained some propaganda support for a time from the Castro regime, but even with Cuban backing it was unable to develop an effective political organization.

Cuba

The position of the party in Cuba is unique among the Communist parties of Latin America. It is by far the most powerful Communist organization in the Western Hemisphere, but technically it does not exist. On the surface the party lost its separate identity in mid-1961, when it was absorbed into the Integrated Revolutionary Organizations, a mass political body which served as the intermediary stage in the construction of the United Party of the Socialist Revolution. In March 1962 Castro revealed that the new political grouping was in effect an expansion of the Communist party, and despite his criticism of this state of affairs Communists continue to be the dominant faction in it. The inclusion of the Communist party in the state political apparatus came about as the result of circumstances peculiar to the Cuban revolution. Only a Castro-type revolution in another country will indicate whether this organizational pattern is regarded as desirable for Communists elsewhere in Latin America.

Who Are the Communists?

THE COMMUNIST PARTIES OF LATIN AMERICA CLAIM TO BE THE VAN-
guard of the proletariat. The primary purpose of the party, in
the Communist view, is to awaken the political consciousness of
the proletariat, to inspire it to political action, and to lead it to
political power. The Communists maintain incessantly that only
they understand and care about the grievances of the lower class
and are capable of forming a government that will satisfy these
grievances. It is in the nature of things, according to the Communists, that the upper class and the middle class exist only by
exploiting the proletariat. Thus, with rare exceptions, members
of the upper and middle classes can not appreciate and will not
alleviate the plight of the lower stratum of society. Any real
improvement in the lot of the masses must be accomplished by
the masses themselves, working through and in support of their
Communist party. This is the line that recurs constantly in
propaganda and recruitment campaigns of the Latin American
Communist parties.

The implication in the Communist claims and reasoning is
clear. The Communist party is, and must be, composed overwhelmingly of members drawn from the working class. This
implication is highly misleading when not completely erroneous.
It has never been more than partially true anywhere in Latin
America.

The fiction that the communist parties are predominantly
of, as well as for, the proletariat is one that the Communists have
assiduously sought to preserve. They have done so largely for
reasons of practical politics and ideological conviction. But, in

addition, they have perpetuated the fiction at least in part because they want to believe it. Marxist-Leninist doctrine holds that the proletariat is peculiarly endowed with the characteristics required of all good Communists. Understandably, those party leaders and members with other social backgrounds have been reluctant to acknowledge that they are perhaps less qualified to be Communists than their lower-class compatriots.

At times they have gone to ridiculous lengths to demonstrate their proletarian proclivities. In the 1920's, for example, the intellectuals and other middle-class members of the Brazilian party affected the habits, mannerisms, and characteristic garb of the city working class in a dramatic effort to show that they were proletarian at heart, if not in origin. A somewhat more sophisticated manifestation of this attitude is the requirement, expressed formally in the statutes of the various parties, that all party members must belong to and participate actively in a trade union, a peasant society, or another appropriate mass organization. If the parties were as proletarian in character as the Communists have insisted, this requirement would seem to be superfluous.

Despite the exaggeration and self-deception evident in their claims, the Communists are sincere in the desire to build the party on a predominantly proletarian base. This was not always the case. In the early years of the movement in Latin America most Communist party leaders plainly held a low opinion of the political level of the working class as a whole. They deliberately sought to create an elite party, separate and distinct from the masses it presumed to lead. This attitude has gradually changed, however, as the lower class has demonstrated a growing capacity to play an active role in national politics. The Communists are more determined than ever to establish the primacy of the party among the lower class, for they recognize that the proletariat is potentially the dominant political force in Latin America. They are still bent on maintaining the party as an elite organization, but they are convinced that it must be clearly identified with the common people. They have found it easy to attribute past mistakes and setbacks to the low level of proletarian consciousness among party leaders or to the party having lost touch with the masses. This line of reasoning has led them to the conclusion that the party must attract a higher proportion of members from the proletariat. Thus, the Communists consistently direct their strongest appeals to the working class of Latin America, particularly to the factory, transport, and maritime workers, who constitute the "true proletariat" in the Marxist view.

Heavy concentration on the urban working class is by no means restricted to the Communists of Latin America. The urban workers were the first to be organized into trade unions and, however reluctantly, to acquire the habit of paying dues. For decades organized labor has been a prime target of most of the political parties, since the party or individual who gains control of the trade unions gains both an important source of funds and a strategically located mass following that can be manipulated for partisan purposes.

The Communists have competed vigorously, and, on the whole, effectively, for positions of leadership in the labor movement. Frequently they have taken the initiative in establishing unions and federations among unorganized workers. Invariably, their objective has been to convert the labor organization into a political appendage of the party and to exploit it to the advantage of the party. In order to achieve this goal, Communist labor leaders have generally been careful to serve the immediate material interests of the union membership. By and large they have proved highly successful in securing the wage and contract benefits demanded by their labor following. They have often been even more effective in claiming responsibility for benefits granted by the government or extracted by labor leaders of other political persuasions. In these ways the Communists have lent credence to their claim that the party is concerned primarily for the welfare of the proletariat.

The response of the Latin American workers to the appeals of communism has varied from time to time and from party to party. As a general rule, during periods of open political activity the parties have absorbed relatively larger numbers of recruits from the working class than from other sectors of the population.

On the other hand, these proletarian members have been among the first to drift away when the party has been repressed. Over the years, however, the proportion of working-class members in the Latin American Communist parties has gradually risen. It is probable that wage earners of all categories now constitute the majority of the rank and file in the Latin American communist movement as a whole. Total party membership, nonetheless, has never represented more than a small fraction of the entire labor movement in any country of Latin America.

Although the Communists might, in theory, prefer to limit their active labor following to the "true proletariat," as practical politicians they have made no serious attempts to do so. They have concentrated heavily on organizing workers in the vital food and service industries in the larger cities, since they recognize that the power to cause or avert strikes in these industries greatly enhances their bargaining position. To facilitate dissemination of the party line, particularly when they do not have open access to the press, radio, and television, the Communists have made a special effort to enlist recruits in the fields of communications and entertainment. These areas have consistently accounted for a disproportionate share of the total party membership.

Some of the most militant working-class supporters of the Communist party have been drawn from outside the urban labor force and from sectors that might not qualify as proletarian in a strict Marxist interpretation. The miners, plantation workers, and petroleum workers in much of Latin America are included in this category. The Communists were among the first to appreciate the political potential of such groups and, although they have not been able to hold all of their original gains, the party is still generally strong in these sectors. The Mexican communist artist David Alfaro Siqueiros organized and led the Miners' Federation of the State of Jalisco in the 1920's, while the nitrate miners of northern Chile have been a bulwark of the Communist party since the days of Luis Emilio Recabarren. Communist labor organizers were the first to win the sympathies of banana-plantation workers in Costa Rica and of oil-field hands in Venezuela. In nearly every other country of Latin America the Communists have drawn support from comparable groups. Despite the range of occupations represented, all these groups share common characteristics that make them attractive to the party. In organization, outlook, and aspirations they resemble the urban proletariat far more than they do the traditional rural lower class. Although they are usually located at some distance from centers of population, they are accessible and are concentrated in relatively large numbers. They receive wages and so are included in the money economy. In the great majority of instances they are employed by foreign companies, principally firms with headquarters in the United States. Thus, they have an identifiable, alien employer who is easily transformed in Communist propaganda into an enemy of the nation and exploiter of the local populace. It is significant that the Communists have generally not been permitted to make important gains among the employees of oil industries owned by the state or of mines and plantations owned by local capitalists. In Cuba, where such enterprises have been nationalized, Communist labor leaders subordinate the interests of the workers to those of the state.

Another of the myths that the Communists are now seeking to convert into reality is the long-standing claim that the party represents the peasants of Latin America. Since the day of the feeble "worker-peasant blocs" in the mid-1920's, Communists have been proclaiming their intention to establish governments of workers and peasants, implying that the two groups are of equal stature in the eyes of the party. In fact, however, during most of its history the Communist movement in Latin America has shown little interest in the rural lower class. The Communist party, like most other parties in the area, was overwhelmingly urban in composition and outlook. Its leaders were neither able nor willing to sustain the effort required to surmount geographical and psychological barriers separating them from the peasantry. The principal obstacle was their inability to communicate with the illiterate and apathetic rural masses, who played little if any role in national politics and whose expectations for change were even lower than their standard of living.

In the two decades before World War II the Communists of Latin America had an excellent opportunity to build a peasant following, for few other political groups were paying any attention to the rural masses. Yet, only for a brief moment in El Salvador, and in Mexico where indigenous revolutionary groups had already aroused the hopes and political awareness of the peasantry, did the Communists encounter even temporary success in creating a peasant-party apparatus. In the rest of the area their indifference and inability to comprehend the peasant mentality prevented them from generating enthusiasm for the party among the rural lower class.

Since the second world war several factors have coincided to bring about a gradual change in the condition of the peasants and the Communist attitude toward them. Considerable improvements in transportation and communications have served to reduce the physical and intellectual isolation of many rural communities, while in most countries parties of the center and left have launched competing campaigns to incorporate the rural inhabitants into the political life of the nation. Within the Communist movement a few prominent figures were inspired by the victory of the peasant-based Communist party in China, and suggested that the Latin American parties might well draw valuable lessons from the Chinese experience. The Guatemalan Communists sought openly to create a Chinese-style armed peasant force in the latter rays of the Arbenz regime, and the Brazilian party began sending a few organizers into rural districts at about the same time. On the whole, however, the Latin American Communists remained largely indifferent to the rural masses until the success of Castro's revolution in Cuba.

The Cuban example demonstrated to the satisfaction of Communists and other leftists throughout the area that a revolutionary movement using guerrilla tactics and appealing to the recently aroused aspirations of the peasants could come to power against overwhelming odds in Latin America. The fact that peasants did not play a decisive role in the essentially urban, middle-class revolt against Batista was widely ignored, inasmuch as Castro initially claimed—and was believed—to have led a successful agrarian-based revolution. In any case, it quickly became evident that the promise of wholesale land reform and a dramatic rise in social status have an almost irresistible appeal to the landless throughout Latin America. The ease with which the Cuban Communist party seized credit for and substantial control over the Cuban revolution gave the Latin American Communists a tremendous psychological boost. Since 1959, inspired by what they believe the Cuban model to be, Communists in most of the region have been sustaining a concerted drive to win a mass rural following, attempting to take over existing peasant organizations and to establish new ones.

In the present situation, therefore, the party has both a genuine interest in the peasants and an appeal certain to excite their expectations. But the opportunity to pose convincingly as the only saviour of the downtrodden-peasant masses has passed. After generations of neglect the peasants may now choose among a broad range of parties, all employing virtually the same demagogic approach. This situation may facilitate Communist penetration of peasant groups organized by other parties, but it hampers Communist recruitment efforts in the rural areas. Under the circumstances, in spite of the attention the Communist party belatedly lavishes on them, peasants still account for only an insignificant minority in the Latin American Communist movement.

In Communist demonology the middle class—the despised *bourgeoisie*—is the first and foremost enemy of the people. The Latin American Communists have consistently echoed the approved Marxist-Leninist preachments on the evils of the middle class, haranguing against "bourgeois mentality," ridiculing "bourgeois morality," satirizing middle-class concern for the rights of the individual, and denouncing "bourgeois greed for profits" at the expense of the proletariat. Since the movement began in Latin America the publications of every Communist party and the public statements of every prominent Communist spokesman have been riddled with such phrases. Yet, virtually every Communist party in Latin America has drawn most of its effective leaders and its most militant members from the very class that it professes to hold in contempt.

This obvious disparity between theory and application causes the Communists little public concern. The same Marxism-Leninism which teaches hatred for the *bourgeoisie* has supplied the formulas for rationalizing inconsistency between word and practice. In the first place, it is accepted that class origin per se does not bar an individual from membership in the party. Any person, regardless of social background, may be qualified to become a Communist, provided he is capable of placing the interests of the masses above his class interests and personal welfare. Within the broad limits of Marxist-Leninist doctrine, moreover, the expression "bourgeoisie" is subject to somewhat elastic interpretation. In response to practical situations that have faced Communist parties everywhere, international Communist theoreticians have found it necessary and convenient to refine and re-define the term to meet the political exigencies of the moment. Contempt and suspicion of the middle class remain a central tenet of Marxism-Leninism, but some sectors of the middle class are clearly more contemptible than others. In practice the individual Communist parties in Latin America are allowed considerable latitude in recruiting from and cooperating with segments of the *bourgeoisie,* as immediate circumstances dictate.

The Latin American Communists tend to classify the various sectors of the *bourgeoisie* primarily according to size and source of income. In general, the higher the income, the higher the level of resistance and opposition to the party, but when further distinction must be drawn the source of an individual's wealth is more significant than the amount. A middle-income landlord, for example, might well be more hostile to the party than the owner of a large manufacturing plant.

In the Communist view the *petit bourgeois* white-collar workers are the most attractive, or least suspect, sector of the middle class. This sector includes employees in commercial firms, school teachers, bank workers, medium- and low-level bureaucrats, and others whose income is derived from modest salaries rather than from property. The *petit bourgeoisie* is regarded as the middle-class element closest to the masses—and therefore extremely susceptible to communist appeals—because it suffers from the same economic pressures that oppress the proletariat. This group appears to provide the bulk of the middle-class membership in the Communist parties of Latin America.

Comparable in economic status but much less reliable politically, from the Communist point of view, are the small shopkeepers and artisans whose clientele is drawn chiefly from low-income groups. For although this sector's standard of living places it on substantially the same level with wage earners and low-salaried employees, it is capitalistic in that its livelihood depends on profits. In most respects it shares the economic plight of the proletariat and can be expected to endorse at least some of the political objectives of the Communist party. In a few of the smaller parties, such as those of Central America, this lower–middle-class element accounts for a significant portion of the total membership.

Artists, intellectuals, professionals, and higher-level bureaucrats comprise a separate small sector of the *bourgeoisie* that has always been a prime target of the Latin American Communist parties. The individuals in this group ordinarily have several occupations and sources of income, including private practice, university professorships, positions in government agencies, and investments in real estate. Thus, they are capitalists by definition, but their income is seldom derived directly from what the Communists call "monopoly capitalism." In Communist eyes they have the great advantage of being deeply concerned with questions of social justice, economic development, and national sovereignty, while their lack of ties with large national and foreign enterprises permits them to view national problems "realistically." Relatively more individuals from this group than from any other sector of the middle class are responsive to the appeals of communism. The bulk of these remain outside the party but participate actively in Communist-front organizations. The select few who become party militants account for much of the leadership of every Communist party in Latin America. As a general rule, at least half the Communist leadership is from this group, and the proportion is higher in the smaller parties.

The Communists divide the remainder of the Latin American middle class into two broad categories, distinguished by attitude toward "imperialism" rather than by economic status. The first, which they call the "national *bourgeoisie*," is comprised largely of owners and managers of firms that compete against foreign imports and foreign-owned enterprises in Latin America. The Communists regard this "patriotic" sector as at best a temporary and vacillating ally, since it is opposed to any significant change in the condition of the proletariat. It can ordinarily be expected, however, to support ultranationalistic campaigns and demands for expanded trade with the Soviet bloc. This sector contains a large percentage of the anonymous "friends of the party," who are an important source of funds for the Communist movement, but it provides few active sympathizers and virtually no recruits to the party anywhere in Latin America.

The second group is the *entreguista* middle class, so-called for its alleged willingness to "hand over" the resources and sovereignty of Latin America to "Yankee imperialism."[1] In the Communist analysis of Latin America society, this minority group shades imperceptibly into the "reactionary" upper class of bankers, large industrialists, merchants in the import-export trade, and large landowners. On occasion it is possible for the party to take advantage of "secondary contradictions" between elements of this group and their imperialist allies, but on the whole it is regarded as the implacable enemy of the party and of the masses. Even this group, nonetheless, includes friends of the party, who seem to look upon contributions to the Communist movement as a form of insurance.

It is significant that a sector which has supplied much of the leadership of the Latin American Communist parties is rarely described by Communists in terms of class origin or social status. This sector is comprised of university students, one of the most

---

1. The expression *entreguista*, used in both Spanish America and Brazil, is derived from the verb *entregar*, to hand over or surrender. As employed by Communists it has a highly derogatory meaning tantamount to treason.

articulate and politically alert elements of Latin American society. Although students in Latin America are drawn preponderantly from upper- and middle-class families, the Communists assume, on the whole correctly, that during their student years their political attitudes and actions will not be determined primarily by financial or class interests. Rather, their highly developed nationalism, their sensitivity to social and economic injustice, and the long tradition of student participation in politics will make them prone to use political action to change the *status quo.* In the Communist view, while they are students they are opponents of the classes from which they come. This characteristic sets them apart, if only temporarily, from the rest of society and gives them an importance to the Communists on a par with that of workers and peasants.

In actual fact, only a small minority of the university-student body in Latin America has ever subscribed fully to the Communist program for social, economic, and political change. This small group, however, has consistently been large enough to serve as a reservoir of potential Communist party leaders throughout the area. At least half the current leaders of the Latin American parties first entered the Communist movement in their student days.

The Latin American Communists have an ambivalent attitude toward the armed forces, whom they regard as another special group outside the usual class structure. They regularly describe the military establishments as organs of repression in the service of the state, even while insisting that these could become "progressive" forces in the "democratic struggle for national liberation." The Communist press is quick to denounce traditional militarism, but praises all indications of military sympathy for the aspirations of the people. In general the Communists feel that the army is the military service closest to the masses and thus most susceptible to the appeals of the party. The victory of Castro's guerrilla forces over the professional army in Cuba has not reduced Communist efforts to attract members from the armed forces in the rest of Latin America.

Through their campaigns against "imperialism" and for

"national emancipation," the Communists appeal to the professional concern of military officers for the defense of national sovereignty and expansion of the national economy. A significant number of ultranationalistic officers in several countries has temporarily, and sometimes inadvertently, made common cause with Communists in "anti-imperialist" propaganda campaigns involving demands for an "independent" foreign policy, nationalization of public utilities and natural resources, or acceptance of Soviet assistance for economic development. A much smaller group, made up chiefly of retired army officers has long been conspicuous in the leadership of a broad range of international Communist-front organizations. Nevertheless, with a few major exceptions, as in El Salvador and Brazil during the 1930's and in Venezuela since 1960, the Communists have failed to persuade commissioned or noncommissioned officers to join them in revolutionary adventures.

Women comprise only a small segment of the total membership of the Latin American Communist parties. This is a matter of continuing concern to party leaders, who emphasize the desirability and need to attract more women into the Communist ranks. Most of the parties maintain several special-interest front organizations designed to appeal to housewives, working women, female students, and women in the professions. Nearly every party has a sprinkling of women in the leadership and, wherever possible, includes women among its candidates for public office. This tendency has been most highly developed in Argentina, Chile, Uruguay, and Brazil, where the participation of women in politics is widely accepted. Even in these countries, however, no more than 10 to 15 per cent of the Communist party members are women.

The foregoing groups and classes of society supply the leaders, members, and sympathizers of the Communist movement throughout Latin America. Thus, even though no two parties are identical in the number or proportion of members from the various social categories, the composition of the movement is remarkably uniform from country to country. The parties are overwhelmingly urban. With rare exceptions the top leadership is comprised of men of middle-class origin and men who have risen to middle-class status. In nearly every instance the great bulk of the membership is drawn from the lower middle class and the upper strata of the working class. Without exception the peasantry contributes only a small percentage of the Communist party rank and file.

The rank-and-file Communists in all parts of Latin America have several basic attitudes in common. They are sufficiently ambitious to be dissatisfied with their lot. They have enough education and awareness of the world around them to realize that their social and economic conditions can be improved. As a result they are impatient for immediate and sweeping change in the *status quo.* These attitudes, of course, are shared by millions of Latin Americans who do not become Communists. The motivations and avowed objectives of Communists and noncommunist leftists are often indistinguishable. The characteristics that set the Communists apart are their complete loss of faith in the democratic process as known in Latin America and their readiness to destroy the established order to achieve their objectives.

Above all, the Communists are a dedicated minority. To a considerable extent their numerical weakness is offset by their high degree of dedication to the cause, willingness to submit to rigid discipline, and subordination of everything else to the party. These qualities make them unique in Latin America. No other party in the area is so demanding of its members or is able to instill in them such a great measure of loyalty and confidence in ultimate victory. In their faith and fanaticism the unreligious Communists are more like members of a zealous missionary order than are the followers of other Latin American political parties.

These qualities, required of all Communist militants, are reinforced at every turn by the party. Every Communist is expected to make communism his way of life, and the demands upon his time and energies are usually such that he must comply or leave the movement. Each Communist, regardless of his position in the party, is expected to be an active member of a cell in his neighborhood or place of employment. In addition, he is expected to contribute dues regularly, to buy and read the party press faithfully, to take part in a continuing round of Marxist-Leninist study groups, and to give unstintingly of his time whenever called upon to perform any of a myriad of party tasks, such as distribution of propaganda leaflets, painting of wall slogans, attendance at public rallies, or participation in street demonstrations, riots, and the like.

It is evident from the Communist record that these high standards have never been fully met by all of the rank and file. Exhortations against apathy and inertia among the members have been a recurrent theme in the party press since the early days of the Communist movement in Latin America. For a variety of reasons the great majority of the recruits that have joined the party in the past four decades have proved unable to sustain the required level of enthusiasm for the Communist cause over a long period of time. There has been a fairly steady loss of members who drifted away out of boredom, because of refusal to follow a sudden reversal of the party line, or to avoid the disadvantages of party membership during the periods of repression. Although attrition has been heaviest among the rank and file, it has affected all levels of the party to a greater or lesser degree. By and large such losses have been compensated by the addition of new members whose hopes and illusions have not yet been dimmed, but over any ten-year period the turnover in party members throughout Latin America has been on the order of 60 per cent. In times of crisis it has been even higher in individual parties. As a result the Communist movement in Latin America is marked by a predominance of young, enthusiastic, and relatively inexperienced members.

Even during periods of extreme repression, a portion of the members has remained constant to form the hard core of the party. These are the Communist militants whose dedication and loyalty have been established beyond question, often in the underground or in exile. They constitute a separate, elite group within the membership and are formally recognized as such in the statutes of some of the parties. The existence of the militant hard core accounts in large part for the accordion-like capacity of the Communist parties to expand or contract rapidly in response to the circumstances of the moment.

The proportion of militants to total membership varies according to the conditions under which the party operates. Ordinarily, when the Communists have legal status or freedom of action, militants represent from one-third to one-tenth of the total. On the other hand, during times of repression, they may account for virtually the entire membership. The experience of the Cuban party is typical in this respect. In the last years of World War II, when the party was claiming some 150,000 followers, only 25,000 were considered militants. By 1958, after serious reverses and five years of illegality, the party was reduced to about twelve thousand active members, practically all of whom qualified as militants. The bulk of those hard-core members who had been jailed, exiled, or otherwise neutralized during the second Batista regime, appear to have resumed active status when party fortunes improved in 1959. This same pattern has recurred in all of the Latin American Communist parties that have exerted even marginal influence in national politics.

In contrast to the continuous process of renewal of rank-and-file members, there has been remarkable continuity in Latin American Communist leadership. The top leaders are predominantly "old" Communists, both in years and experience. The majority of the party presidents, Secretaries-General, and key Central Committee members have been active Communists for twenty-five years or more. In at least six of the parties—those of Argentina, Brazil, Costa Rica, Cuba, Paraguay, and Venezuela —the same individual or clique has held sway for over a quarter of a century, and in Uruguay party-founder Eugenio Gómez dominated for thirty-four years before his ouster in 1955. The record for longevity is shared by Victorio Codovilla and Rodolfo Ghioldi, both of whom in 1963 still led the Argentine party they had founded forty-five years earlier. Other party founders who hold key positions in their organizations are Obdulio Barthe, of Paraguay; Gustavo and Eduardo Machado, of Venezuela; and Manuel Mora, of Costa Rica. These men, and David Alfaro

Siqueiros, titular head of the Mexican party, all entered the Communist movement in the 1920's. A listing of Communists who have played leading roles in the party since the 1930's includes Luiz Carlos Prestes, the Brazilian Communist chief; Luis Corvalán Leppe, Secretary-General of the Chilean party; Gilberto Vieira White, of Colombia; Blas Roca, of Cuba; and Uruguayan party leader Rodney Arismendi. Most of the remaining Latin American Communist leaders rose to prominence in the party during or soon after the second world war.

The disparity between the long tenure of the top leadership and the comparative youth and inexperience of members at lower levels of the party—characteristic of the Communist movement throughout Latin America—is pointed up in the report of the Fourth National Congress of the Communist Party of Brazil. In a sense this Congress, held in November 1954, was a meeting of the party elite, for it excluded all members of less than two years standing and those who did not hold office above the cell level. Yet, even within this select group fewer than one-third of the delegates had been party members for over ten years. The proportions were reversed among Central Committee members, where more than two-thirds had been active in the party for a decade or longer, and well over half had been Communists for at least twenty years. The median age of the delegates was thirty-six years; that of Central Committee members was at least ten years higher. The age gap between leaders and followers has tended to widen since 1954, as many of the members of the Central Committee at that time continue to occupy high posts in the Brazilian party.

The Communist movement in Latin America has attracted leaders of somewhat different backgrounds and widely varying personalities. An indication of the range of diversity among them may be seen in the careers of Victorio Codovilla, Luiz Carlos Prestes, and Blas Roca. Codovilla, an Italian who migrated to Argentina before World War I, was the first important figure to emerge as a leader of Latin American communism. His reputation stems as much from his activities in the international Communist bureaucracy as from his role in the Argentine party.

Codovilla appears to have had no profession or occupation other than that of a paid party official since 1917. His facility for anticipating shifts in the Soviet power structure and for currying favor with the dominant faction in the Kremlin has not been surpassed by any Communist leader in Latin America or elsewhere. As head of the earliest and largest Communist organization in the Western Hemisphere, he soon became the principal Latin American adviser to the Comintern. He was a member of the first Latin American Secretariat in Moscow and Treasurer of that body when it was transferred to Buenos Aires, as the South American Bureau, in 1928. Codovilla went into exile when the Argentine party was suppressed in 1930. He remained out of the country until early in 1941, serving for several years on the Comintern staff in Moscow and as a Comintern agent in Spain during the civil war in that country. In 1940, on his return to Latin America, he is reported to have conveyed Soviet directives for the expulsion of Mexican Communist leaders, Valentín Campa and Hernán Laborde. Following the revolution of 1943, Codovilla was again exiled—this time to Chile—but returned to Argentina in 1945. In the postwar period Codovilla has usually represented the Argentine party at international Communist gatherings. Probably because of his frequent absences, he has not held the office of Secretary-General of the party for many years, but continues to dominate the Communist movement in Argentina from his position on the party's Executive Bureau.

Luiz Carlos Prestes, of Brazil, is unique among Latin American communist leaders in that he has a military background and had earned a national reputation as a revolutionary before he became a Communist. Born in 1898, the son of an army captain who died shortly thereafter, Prestes was raised in poverty. He graduated from the military academy with honors in 1918 but did not attract public notice until 1924, when he led a rebel column on a prolonged campaign through the Brazilian hinterland seeking to inspire a popular revolution. Although he failed in his objective and went into exile in 1927, Prestes gained nationwide fame and the sobriquet Knight of Hope, which he carried with him into the Communist camp three years later.

Refusing an offer of amnesty by the new Brazilian government, in 1931 he went to the Soviet Union, where he remained for about four years being groomed for his future role as head of the Communist movement in Brazil. He returned to Brazil in 1935 to direct the left-wing National Liberation Alliance and the ill-fated uprising against the Vargas regime in November of that year. Prestes was captured and sent to prison, where he languished for nine years, until he was released under a general amnesty in 1945. During the two years that the party enjoyed legal status, Prestes supervised its highly successful recruitment drive and was largely responsible for attracting half a million votes for party candidates in the elections of 1945 and 1947. He won the only Communist seat in the Senate, which he held until January 1948, when the mandates of all Communists in public office were canceled. Prestes then went underground for a decade but maintained close control over the clandestine party and represented it periodically at international Communist meetings. When he emerged from obscurity in 1958 to lend support to a flagging electoral campaign, it was soon evident that his popular appeal had waned. Within the party, however, he has retained full authority and the loyalty of the rank and file. Opponents who challenged his leadership in 1957 and 1960 have been systematically isolated and expelled. There are indications that over the years Prestes has had somewhat more freedom than other Latin American Communist leaders to modify Soviet directives to meet local conditions. Nonetheless, he has never pursued a course opposed to current Soviet foreign-policy objectives, regardless of the immediate impact on the Brazilian party.

Blas Roca is one of the few top Latin American Communists drawn from the proletariat. He was born Francisco Calderío, of a working-class family in Manzanillo, Cuba, in 1908. He joined the Communist party before 1930 and distinguished himself as a labor activist. He took the name Blas Roca—his favorite alias in the Communist underground—before becoming Secretary-General of the party in 1934. Roca's elevation to the highest post in the party at age twenty-six appears to have been arranged by Fabio Grobart, the Comintern agent delegated to purge the

Cuban Communist organization following its poor showing in the 1933 revolution. His rapid rise in international Communist circles was marked in 1935 by his appointment as an alternate member of the Comintern's Executive Committee. In Soviet eyes he apparently ranked with Rodolfo Ghioldi—the only other Latin American among the alternate members—next to Luiz Carlos Prestes, who was a full member of the Executive Committee. An excellent organizer and flexible tactician, Roca has proved worthy of Soviet confidence. In the three decades of his reign he has converted the inconsequential Communist party into a cohesive political force through rigid discipline and timely cooperation with Cuban strong men Fulgencio Batista and Fidel Castro. Communist gains during the first Batista regime—legal status, control of organized labor, and a voice in national affairs —have now been overshadowed by the success of Roca's policy of apparent subordination to Fidel Castro. With the incorporation of the party into Castro's United Party of the Socialist Revolution, Roca has formally surrendered leadership of the Communists to the Cuban dictator. He remains, however, on the directorate of the new political body and a prominent spokesman for Cuban communism in international Communist circles.

The similarities between the Latin American Communist leaders are more striking than the characteristics that distinguish them from each other. Without exception the leaders of the Latin American parties are professional Communists in the full meaning of the expression. They have been trained in the Soviet Union, and many of them have served for prolonged periods as officials in the international Communist bureaucracy in Latin America or Europe. They are steeped in Marxist-Leninist doctrine and have learned to interpret every political development affecting their country or the party in Marxist-Leninist terms. For the sake of their political convictions they have endured oppression, imprisonment, and exile from their native land. More significantly, they have survived drastic purges and dramatic reversals and counterreversals of international Communist policy. They occupy positions of leadership because they have proved adept at anticipating and rationalizing Soviet-dictated departures

116 INTERNATIONAL COMMUNISM IN LATIN AMERICA

from past Communist policies and at making such departures palatable to the rank and file. Within the limits of Marxist-Leninist doctrine, as formulated at any particular time by the head of the Communist Party of the Soviet Union, the Latin American leaders have shown themselves to be completely flexible—so much so that their enemies accuse them of an absolute lack of political principles. Yet, they have been inflexible in refusing every opportunity to reject Soviet tutelage or to withdraw from the international movement, even when such actions appeared to serve the immediate interests of the local party. In short, their careers are fully identified with the international Communist movement as directed by the Soviet Union.

Organization of the Party

DISCIPLINED ORGANIZATION IS THE GREATEST ASSET OF THE LATIN American Communist parties. It has permitted them to survive long periods of repression, to operate underground or in the open, and to contract or expand rapidly, as circumstances dictate. Throughout Latin America the several Communist parties all have the same basic structure, patterned closely after that of the Communist Party of the Soviet Union. Although strategy, tactics, and immediate objectives have changed—sometimes drastically—in the past four decades, the party organization has not been fundamentally altered since the first Communist groups were established in the area.

"COLLECTIVE LEADERSHIP" VS. FACTIONALISM

In theory the Communist parties of Latin America operate on the parallel principles of "democratic centralism" and "collective leadership." The first of these holds that all policy decisions affecting the members, operations, and objectives of the party are to be reached through free and open debate at all levels. Once approved by the majority, decisions so reached must be accepted by the entire membership. Under "collective leadership," executive and administrative action are to be determined and agreed upon in advance by a majority of the elected officers at the appropriate level of the party. Thus, theoretically, the party is an autonomous, cohesive unit directed by committees which carry out the freely expressed will of the majority of its members. Invariably the statutes describe the party as "monolithic," a term which implies identity of views throughout.

117

In practice, no Communist party in Latin America has ever approached this ideal. The parties, as suggested in the statutes, are indeed highly centralized, but with a rigid hierarchy in which authority and command flow in fact from the top down. Collective leadership has been the rare exception rather than the rule in Latin America, functioning only for brief periods in a few parties in the course of internal power struggles. The persistence of factionalism suggests that there has seldom been full or continuing agreement on strategy and tactics in any Latin American party. The membership at large, moreover, has never determined basic policies. Occasionally these are fixed and transmitted to the party by the leaders of the international movement. More often they are determined, without specific directives, by local party officials in response to policy indicators appearing in international Communist propaganda and news media. The smaller parties may also receive guidance on policy from the heads of stronger Communist organizations in neighboring countries. The Haitian and Dominican Communists, for instance, have frequently looked to the Cuban party for direction, while instructions to the parties in Central America have customarily been channeled through the Communist party in Mexico.

PYRAMIDAL STRUCTURE

The Communist party structure may be described as a pyramid in which the national leadership forms the apex and local units, or cells, make up the broad base. Some of the smaller parties have in descending order only national, state, municipal, and local divisions, while the more highly developed ones and those in the larger countries usually include regional, zone, and district commands as well. The number, designation, and hierarchical order of the echelons in the Communist command structure vary from party to party, but in each case are clearly stipulated in the statutes. Changes in the vertical structure are rare. In contrast, the number of units in each echelon below the national level is highly flexible, subject to bellows-like expansion or contraction with changing party fortunes. This horizontal flexi-

bility, which enables the party to absorb thousands of new
recruits at one time and to withstand a sudden dramatic loss
of members at another, is the great organizational strength of
the Communist movement in Latin America.

The subdivisions of the Communist party are for the most
part established on a geographic basis; however, where feasible
provision is made for the creation of intermediate commands
on a professional or occupational basis as well. In the Brazilian
party, for example, railroad and maritime workers are included
under separate regional organisms which have nationwide jurisdiction. Communist cells are regularly set up in residential
neighborhoods and in places of employment, at the convenience
of the party. Most of the Latin American parties have cells of
both categories.

National Congress

According to the party statutes, the supreme authority of the
Communist organization in each country is the *National Congress*. Ordinarily it is to meet every two or three years, when
convoked by the Central Committee. As a practical matter no
Communist party in Latin America has been able to hold National Congresses consistently at the intervals specified in its
statutes. In the case of the Brazilian party, twenty-five years
elapsed between its Third and Fourth Congresses and another
six years passed before the Fifth National Congress met in 1960.
In that same year in Cuba—where the Party Congress is called
the *National Assembly*—the eighth meeting was held after a
lapse of eight years. The Communists in Honduras were unable
to convoke a National Congress until 1958. At the other extreme
the Chilean Communists met for the twelfth time and the Uruguayan party held its Eighteenth National Congress in 1962.

The National Congress is comprised of delegates elected by
the conferences at the next lower level of the party and distributed numerically according to a formula determined by the Central Committee. In most instances the delegates must be party
militants of several years standing. In Colombia, for example,
three years militancy is required except in the case of factory

workers, who may be elected as delegates to the Party Congress after two years.

The power of the National Congress is more apparent than real. According to the party statutes, it has four principal responsibilities. These are: first, to determine the party's tactical line on current political issues; second, at irregular intervals, to revise the official program and statutes; third, to hear and approve the reports of the Central Committee; and fourth, to elect members and alternate members to that body. In connection with the latter function, the National Congress is ordinarily the agency which disciplines those members who have clashed with the top leadership.

On those rare occasions when a Congress is held while a power struggle is taking place within Communist ranks, the assembled delegates may actually exercise the initiative with which they are charged in the statutes. As a practical matter, however, it is seldom that a Latin American Communist Party Congress produces surprising or startling results. For not less than two months preceding the Congress all problems and materials to be considered by the delegates must be thoroughly discussed at each echelon of the party on the basis of documents prepared by the Central Committee. Under the circumstances, the National Congress is usually well rehearsed and serves merely as a rubber stamp, sanctioning decisions and actions already taken by the Central Committee or the dominant faction in it.

National Conference

Most of the Latin American Communist parties also provide for a *National Conference,* which may be convoked by the Central Committee to consider urgent political matters in the interval between Party Congresses. The National Conference is more restricted in size and authority than the National Congress, but it may serve much the same purpose. In practice the Latin American Communists have most often used the Party Conference as a substitute for the National Congress during periods when the party is severely repressed. For a clandestine party the Conference has the distinct advantage of a relatively small number of delegates who can be summoned and dispersed quickly in order to escape detection by the police. Decisions taken by the Conference must be ratified by the Central Committee before they are mandatory for the party membership.

Central Committee

Nominally, between meetings of the Communist Party Congress the maximum authority resides in the *Central Committee.* This body, which is sometimes known as the *National Committee,* always includes the top party leaders and often the ranking secondary figures as well. The size of the Central Committee is usually determined by the size of the party, with the number of full members being roughly equivalent to the number of committees at the next lower level. Full members are generally expected to have highly developed organizational abilities and demonstrated competence in at least one major field of Communist activity. Some personal differences are tolerated among members, but candidates known to be strongly opposed to the current line of the top leadership are seldom elected. The only statutory requirement for election to the Central Committee, however, is continuous active membership in the party for a specified period. The minimum is never less than two years. It is more often three years, and some parties require five. In practice most Central Committee members in the Latin American parties have been active Communists for at least a decade. The ranks of alternate members of the Central Committee may include able younger men who have displayed leadership qualities at intermediate party commands, former full members who have been demoted, and occasionally a few mediocrities whose chief distinction is long and loyal service in the Communist cause. Frequently the head of the Communist youth organization is also an alternate member of the Central Committee.

The Central Committee has an impressive array of formal functions, which are carefully stipulated in the party statutes. Its major duties include responsibility for carrying out the decisions of the Party Congress, supervising party finances, enforcing observance of the party program and statutes, directing and controlling the Communist press and other propaganda media, and fixing the number of positions on each subordinate committee. In some parties, moreover, the Central Committee selects from among its members the *central finance commission,* which is directly responsible for fiscal policies and fund-raising activities, and the *central control commission,* which is immediately responsible for dealing with matters of party discipline and security. In countries where Communists may participate in the electoral process, the Central Committee selects party candidates to national public office and decides among lists of candidates to state and municipal posts submitted by the respective committees of the party. By statute the Central Committee is required to meet periodically—usually two or three times per year —and when convoked by a majority of its members. In those parties with legal status or effective freedom of operation, meetings of the Central Committee are customarily held at the statutory intervals. Where the party is rigidly suppressed, plenary sessions of the Central Committee are less frequent and may serve in effect as substitutes for the National Conference and the National Congress.

Executive Bureau—and Aliases

Most of the powers ostensibly held by the Central Committee are actually exercised by the *Executive Bureau.* This select group—which has also been known variously as the *Executive Committee, Political Commission,* and *Presidium*—may range in size from under a dozen to more than twenty men in the Latin American Communist parties. The Executive Bureau is elected by the Central Committee from among its more prominent members, who are normally "old" Communists and trusted lieutenants of the Secretary-General. Often, where the party operates openly, they may be public figures in their own right. In the Brazilian party, for example, during the period of Communist legality in the immediate postwar years eight Executive Bureau members were also congressmen.

The Executive Bureau is formally authorized to direct all activities of the party between meetings of the Central Com mittee. The statutes ordinarily specify that it must report to the Central Committee and be held accountable for its actions. As a practical matter it usually dominates the larger body and, in cooperation with the Secretariat, frequently acts in the name of the Central Committee. The Executive Bureau makes many of the important decisions and originates the bulk of the documents that are attributed to the Central Committee. It has the *de facto* power to decide when a Party Congress or Conference shall be held, to prepare the agenda for the meeting, and to preside over the sessions. The Executive Bureau also has the authority, subject only to subsequent approval by the National Congress, to dissolve or replace any subordinate committee in the party. Such actions by the Executive Bureau are almost invariably approved.

Secretariat

Authority in the Latin American Communist parties is usually concentrated in the *Secretariat,* comprised of the Secretary-General and his most important aides. There are always at least two aides, and the number is often higher, varying according to the size and current situation of the party. In some parties the Secretariat is elected by the Central Committee, in others by the Executive Bureau, but invariably its members are drawn from the latter body. In theory the Secretariat is the administrative staff of the Central Committee or Executive Bureau, responsible for directing the daily-routine operations of the party. In practice it combines staff functions with *de facto* decision-making powers. As a staff organization it regularly transmits decisions of the Central Committee and Executive Bureau to subordinate commands. It also serves, however, in an executive capacity with authority to shift the focus of party activities, to introduce new tactics or modify existing ones, and to transfer members and units within the party. The Secretariat ordinarily is expected to use such powers only to meet urgent situations demanding immediate response by the party leadership. Technically, it is accountable to the Central Committee for its actions. Unless the top leadership is being challenged, however, decisions taken by the Secretariat on its own authority are usually accepted by the party without protest and often without discussion.

Secretary-General

The *Secretary-General* is the highest-elected official and is the dominant personality in most of the Latin American Communist parties. It is significant that the party statutes are silent as to the specific powers and obligations of his office. Ostensibly he derives his authority from the Party Congress, takes decisions in consultation with the Executive Bureau, and is held accountable for his activities at the regular meetings of the Central Committee. Actually his powers stem from the confidence manifested in him by the international Communist leadership. As long as his policies coincide with Soviet designs for the Latin American parties, he can ordinarily rely on the support of the international movement to resist all challenges to his autocratic rule. On the other hand, no Secretary-General who has lost favor with the Soviet leadership has long been able to retain his hold over the party.

The Communist organizations of Argentina and Mexico provide exceptions to the general rule that the Secretary-General is the strongest figure in the party. The Argentine Secretary-General is a figurehead who carries out the orders of Executive Committee member Victorio Codovilla. In Mexico no single individual combined all the traits necessary to assume control when Dionisio Encina was ousted from the top post in 1960 after twenty years in power. The dilemma was resolved at the Thirteenth National Congress by abolishing the office of Secretary-General and replacing it with a triumvirate in which David Alfaro Siqueiros was the most prominent personality.

Party President

A few of the Latin American Communist parties have made provision for the office of *party president*. Nominally it is the highest position in the Communist hierarchy, but in fact it is an honorary post devoid of real authority. In both Cuba and Chile, where the office long existed, it was created to accommodate an important Communist personality, still useful to the party and well liked by the rank and file but no longer acceptable as a top executive officer.

Assemblies

At each of the intermediate echelons of the Communist party there are *conferences*—sometimes known as *assemblies*—and corresponding *executive committees.* The formal duties of these conferences are usually detailed in the party statutes. They include discussion and resolution of problems submitted for their consideration by higher authorities, e.g., supervision over the ideological instruction and training of members of the respective executive committees and finance and control commissions, and the election of delegates to the conference at the next higher level of the party. The executive committees are responsible for directing routine party business within the area under their jurisdiction, for executing the decisions of the conference, and for transmitting and carrying out directives received from upper echelons. Subordinate units are required by statute to meet more frequently than those with larger jurisdictions. In most of the Latin American parties the conference immediately above the cell level is expected to meet at least once monthly.

Cells or Base Organizations

Every Communist in Latin America, regardless of his office or standing in the movement, is ordinarily required to belong to one of the *party cells.* These are often called *base organizations,* and in Cuba are designated *Socialist committees,* but uniformly they are the basic organizational unit—the grass roots of the party. It is here that new members are recruited and contacts are established and maintained with sympathizers and friends of the party. Almost invariably individual members make their financial contributions and are assigned their specific party tasks at the cell level. Each cell, also, is divided into a conference or assembly, which includes its entire membership, and into an executive body, generally known as the secretariat. The cell assembly is required to meet frequently, usually at weekly or bi-

weekly intervals, to discuss its assignments, to assess its performance, and to organize the study of Marxism-Leninism by the
members. The cell secretariat includes at least three officers
and may have as many as seven, elected by acclamation. Cells
may be created at places of work or in residential districts,
wherever there are three or more party members. As the membership increases the cell may be subdivided into sections, each
with a representative in the secretariat, or it may be dissolved
and re-created as two or more separate cells.

Special Cells

The Communist party cell is ordinarily established by au-
thorization of the next higher committee, which retains immediate supervision over it. Numerous exceptions occur, however, because of Communist emphasis on recruiting urban
industrial laborers. The statutes usually provide that special
"industrial" or "enterprise" cells shall be set up in factories and
other industrial plants employing a large number of workers.
These special cells are sometimes created in the normal fashion
by the immediately superior committee, but often they are authorized by and remain directly subordinate to committees at a
much higher level in the party hierarchy. In the Brazilian party,
for example, enterprise cells in plants employing more than five
hundred men are under the jurisdiction of regional committees.
In some of the smaller parties the Central Committee itself may
create and supervise industrial cells.

Party Fractions

Most of the Latin American Communist parties require all
members to take active part in an appropriate trade union, peasant organization, professional association, or front group. In
such organizations, where party cells do not already exist, the
Communists are expected to form small nuclei known as *party
fractions,* which have most of the duties and obligations of cells.
The primary purpose of fractions is to disseminate the Communist line and to attract new members to the party. As the fractions
increase in size, they are normally converted into cells. Active

membership in a party fraction does not relieve the individual Communist of his obligation to participate in regular cell activities.

Youth Auxiliary

In many of the Latin American countries the Communists maintain a youth auxiliary which is technically separate from the party but serves in fact as an adjunct to it. The Communist youth movement closely resembles the party in structure, with conferences and executive committees at national, intermediate, and local levels. The rank and file are not initially required to be Marxists, but they are subjected to intensive indoctrination and are encouraged to transfer to the party at age eighteen. Usually membership in the Communist youth precludes simultaneous membership in the party, except that officers at intermediate and higher levels are often active Communists and in some instances sit as alternate or ex officio members of corresponding committees of the party. The chief functions of the Communist youth are to organize the "progressive" youth of the country to disseminate the party line, particularly on issues of interest to young people, to reinforce the Communist party by attendance at public rallies and protest meetings, and, where possible, to act as the vanguard of a broad regional or national youth movement.

Strategy, Tactics, and Techniques

THE TIGHTLY KNIT PARTY WITH ITS YOUTH WING IS THE INDISPEN-
sable nucleus of the Latin American Communist movement. In
most of the area, however, the party is but a small and separate
segment of the total Communist apparatus. The existence of a
broad Communist movement in addition to the party testifies to
the success of two mutually reinforcing campaigns long pursued
by the Latin American Communists. These are to build a manip-
ulatable mass following outside the party and to create a favorable, or at least tolerant, attitude toward themselves and their
objectives among opinion-molding sectors of the population. The
tactics and techniques employed in these campaigns have varied
over the years according to local circumstances and to changing
directives received from international Communist leaders, but
the basic strategy has been remarkably consistent since the mid-
1930's. The Communists have greatly extended their voice and
audience by establishing or seizing control of mass groups, such
as organized labor and student societies, by creating and directing
a wide variety of front groups, and by penetrating organizations
which influence public and official opinion. They have applied
their organizational skills in each of these spheres, which they
exploit as propaganda vehicles for the party. Although each of
the Communist-led mass organs and front groups includes party
members, the Communists are scrupulous in avoiding formal
organizational ties between these bodies and the party itself.

From the beginning the Communists have directed more attention toward penetration and control of the labor movement
than to any other mass organization in Latin America. They

have been encouraged in this strategy both by their desire to attract working-class members into the party and by the conviction that control of organized labor is a necessary first step in the eventual acquistion of political power. The creation of a solid labor base also carries with it more immediate and practical benefits to the party. Once in command of key labor offices, Communists have access to funds which they can divert to party purposes. They are able to present the current Communist line as the views of the trade-union membership. And they can impose on their trade-union following policies determined by the local Communist party or leaders of the international movement.

Where the party is illegal, all Communists in the labor movement attempt to disguise their political affiliation. Elsewhere, at the discretion of the party, they may operate openly, but in all cases their techniques are similar. Not only do they recruit and organize new members for the party, but they actively solicit positions of leadership in the trade unions and election as delegates to municipal, state, and national labor bodies. Because Communist labor leaders are paid by the party, and hence can devote full time to their labor duties, they have a decided advantage over noncommunist rivals for unremunerated trade-union posts. Sometimes their candidacy in not contested. But even when there is opposition a Communist cell is still frequently able to gain effective control over a trade union by filibustering and by other means generally prolonging discussion at union meetings until the noncommunists leave in disgust.

When they have a foothold at the trade-union level, the Communists try to extend their control to all organized workers in the nation. In the past—and even yet in countries where the labor movement is poorly organized—Communists have played an active role in forming federations of trade unions in related crafts and industries. In each case they have sought to dominate or to exert strong influence over such federations. Once two or more of these have been established, they usually urge the consolidation of all federations into a single, unified national labor body. Outside of Cuba, where Communists hold virtually all of the top labor positions, this policy has had perhaps its most complete and enduring success in Chile. There Communists long influenced and for several years have openly dominated the central labor confederation. Where they are unable to capture an existing national confederation, the Communists consistently advocate the creation of a new one, even if it is in fact only a paper organization. Their objective is to fragment strong noncommunist labor groupings and to unify those under Communist command. In Uruguay, after repeated failures to take over the Socialist-led labor confederation, Communists in 1961 set up the so-called Single Center of Uruguayan Workers and invited all labor organizations, including the rival confederation, to join.

The Latin American Communists have sought persistently, and for a time successfully, to draw the national labor units into a vast regional organization associated with the international Communist labor front. For several years they dominated the only important regional labor confederation in the area. This was the Confederation of Latin American Workers, established in 1938 and led by Vicente Lombardo Toledano, then boss of organized labor in Mexico. Initially it was a legitimate labor central, supported by the major labor confederations of Argentina, Chile, Colombia, Cuba, Ecuador, Peru, Venezuela, and Mexico. From the outset, however, Communist labor leaders were prominent in the Confederation, and their influence increased during World War II, when Communist labor activities were encouraged or tolerated by most of the Latin American governments. Local or national labor groups from fourteen countries were associated with the Confederation in 1944, when Communists gained control of most of the top offices. The take-over was apparently facilitated by Lombardo Toledano, who had been ousted from his Mexican labor post in 1940 and henceforth identified himself increasingly with Communist elements in the international body. With the onset of the cold war in the late 1940's, membership in the Confederation fell off drastically as its noncommunist affiliates withdrew to join either the anticommunist Inter-American Regional Labor Organization or the Association of Latin American Labor Unions, which was promoted by the Perón regime of Argentina. The Confederation was soon little more than a paper organization and propaganda instrument for the communist movement. It affiliated with the communist World Federation of Trade Unions and parroted every theme of the international Communist line, gradually losing prestige in the area until its dissolution was announced in 1962. In that year the Communists attempted to replace the discredited Confederation with a new communist labor front, the Single Center of Latin American Workers, headquartered in Chile. They apparently felt that with a different name and few new faces this front might acquire the power and prestige once commanded by the Confederation of Latin American Workers. The effort failed, however, and for the time being the Confederation is continuing its ineffectual activities.

The pattern of communist tactics and techniques employed in the labor movement is repeated with only slight variations among Latin American youth and student organizations. In these areas the Communists are somewhat more prone to operate openly, even in countries where the party is proscribed, although they disguise or minimize their political connections when circumstances dictate. Again, material support received from local and international Communist sources frequently gives Communist activists an advantage over young leaders from other political parties. The Communists concentrate their efforts largely at the university level, but they also attempt to seize or organize separate secondary-school student associations and urban and rural youth groups wherever possible. They seek to infiltrate and win converts in all such groups, to obtain direct or indirect control over the key offices, to create or capture the national organization of each of the separate youth and student associations, and then to draw all these into a broad national body under Communist domination or influence. In most instances the Communists prefer to elect a sympathizer or useful innocent to the top national post in order to reserve avowed or disguised party members for such positions as Treasurer and Secretary of Propaganda. At each level Communist-led and Communist-influenced organizations are used as forums for discussing and disseminating Communist propaganda themes, which are invariably presented as the independent views of all youth and students in the country. Where the Communists are in control the national associations are affiliated with the Cuban-based, Latin American youth and student movements and with such international Communist fronts as the International Union of Students and the World Federation of Democratic Youth.

The effectiveness of Communist tactics and propaganda in Latin America depends largely on the existence of a wide range of interlocking front groups that supplement and draw upon the Communist-led mass organizations. Therefore, the Communists always attempt to penetrate and manipulate women's organizations, professional societies, cultural associations, ethnic groups, and other special-interest groups, employing specific appeals to each. Usually the special-interest fronts emphasize some legitimate need or particular aspiration of the group, such as higher wages, agrarian reform, benefits to students, the rights of youth, or equal rights for women, but they soon extend their activities beyond these limited socioeconomic objectives to engage in political propaganda. Nominally, these groups are separate, autonomous entities, although in fact the key offices in substantially all fronts within each country are held by the same small clique of disguised Communists, sympathizers, and fellow travelers. Wherever possible this leadership core is supplemented by useful innocents—both prominent noncommunist personalities attracted by the avowed objectives of specific front organizations and professional joiners who reappear as figureheads in front after front. The useful innocents provide a façade to mask the organizations' links with the party.

The situation in Guatemala during the period of Communist ascendancy in the early 1950's provides a clear example of the kind and range of mass-based front groups the Communists strive to exploit. There the organizations under Communist domination included the General Confederation of Workers of Guatemala, the National Peasant Confederation of Guatemala, the Guatemalan Women's Alliance, the Alliance of Democratic Youth of Guatemala, the Democratic University Front, the Confederation of Secondary School Students, and the Saker-Ti Group of Young Artists and Writers.

The various mass-based groups either are united under a broad national front or are deployed separately to support appeals that cut across class and group lines. International themes include "peace," "democracy," "abolition of nuclear weapons," and any other topics currently featured in Soviet propaganda. Local propaganda issues vary somewhat from country to country but are always consistent in at least three respects. They focus on the economic grievances of the broadest sectors of the population, they oppose the political moderation conducive to orderly national development, and they encourage emotional anti-United States nationalism. Thus, Communist fronts throughout Latin America in recent years have protested against "the high cost of living," and called for "defense of national sovereignty" against alleged "Yankee imperialism," "nationalization of large landholdings," "nationalization of natural resources," "expropriation of foreign-owned utilities," and "defense of the Cuban revolution."

Most of the major front organizations are based upon legitimate-interest groups which would exist regardless of Communist involvement in them. In addition to these the Communists also maintain a constantly changing array of contrived-front groups, each ostensibly nonpolitical and created to support a particular propaganda theme or an objective of the local party or of the international movement. A few are preserved as regular features of the Communist apparatus even though they may be ineffectual. For example, there has been at least one "peace" front, affiliated with the Communist World Peace Council, in nearly every Latin American country since the late 1940's. For the most part, however, those fronts that fail to invoke a popular response are soon dropped, although they are rarely dissolved and may be revived later at the convenience of the party to lend added support to some new theme or objective. On occasion one of these fronts sparks the imagination of the public and achieves national significance for a time. In such circumstances the entire Communist propaganda machine concentrates on this front, which expands in size and scope until it is suppressed by the regime or until Communist interests shift to another subject.

One of the most successful of the contrived fronts was established in Brazil in 1947. Its purpose was to promote pressure for nationalization of the petroleum industry. Local units set up in the larger cities were brought together under a National Executive Committee for the Defense of Petroleum. Even before the state petroleum corporation, *Petrobrás,* was created by the Brazilian government in 1953, the objectives of the petroleum front had been broadened to include demands for state control over other natural resources, electric power, and basic industries. The coordinating body of the enlarged front was called the National Executive Committee for the Defense of Petroleum and the National Economy. In 1954 this front organization, now with further ultranationalistic objectives, was converted into the League for National Emancipation. The League became increasingly critical of the Kubitschek administration, which abolished it in 1956, but not until the Communists had succeeded in encouraging and identifying themselves with the rising tide of Brazilian nationalism.

The continuing proliferation of front organizations is a characteristic of the Communist movement throughout Latin America. It is a technique consciously employed to create the impression of widespread, spontaneous, and growing enthusiasm for the issues and objectives propounded by the local Communist party. As a matter of fact the great majority of the contrived fronts and many of the supposedly mass-based front groups are actually paper organizations with minimal membership and little or no resonance among the public they claim to represent. The sheer number of front organizations, however, serves in large measure to compensate for their individual weaknesses and to further the illusion the Communists seek to project.

The Latin American Communist parties use all their front groups somewhat as echo chambers to magnify and distort the apparent volume of popular support for the particular themes which each one emphasizes. The leaders and ranking members of supposedly unrelated fronts sign each other's petitions, en-

dorse each other's slogans, and take part in each other's public
gatherings. This pattern has been consistent since the formation
of the first Communist fronts in the area and has involved increasing numbers of organizations since the second world war. In
Brazil, for example, at least fifteen different front organizations
were included among the formal sponsors of a so-called "congress
for the defense of petroleum" in 1955, while delegates from
another score of fronts attended the sessions and approved the
final resolutions. In mid-1962 a Communist-inspired "anti-
Fascist" demonstration in Montevideo was attended by some
five hundred people representing over ninety different organizations. Half of the latter were clearly Communist or Communist-
front groups and many of the others were infiltrated by Communist party members. It is significant that more than twenty
separate fronts "for solidarity with the Cuban revolution" were
represented at the meeting. In recent years pro-Cuba fronts have
become a vital part of the propaganda apparatus of a majority
of the Communist parties of Latin America.

In addition to the allegedly autonomous national and regional front groups, the Communists and their sympathizers
maintain well over one hundred binational "cultural" centers
and friendship societies in at least eleven of the Latin American
republics. These fronts are designed specifically to spread propaganda in favor of closer relations with individual Communist
regimes. A representative listing would include the Institute of
Argentine-Soviet Cultural Relations, the Bolivian-Czechoslovakian Friendship Center, the Brazil-Poland Center of Studies and
University Exchange, the Chilean-East German Cultural Institute, the Colombian Association of Friends of China, the
Mexican-Bulgarian Society of Friendship and Cultural Exchange,
the Peruvian-Rumanian Cultural Institute, and the Uruguayan-
Hungarian Cultural Center. They strive to present themselves as
legitimate expressions of the popular will, concerned with artistic,
educational, literary, and occasionally commercial exchange with
Communist nations. Their connections with the local Communist party are minimized when they cannot be entirely disguised.
With rare exceptions, however, the officers of such organizations

are drawn from the same tight group that provides the leadership of the myriad of Communist fronts throughout Latin America.

The underlying purpose of the binational centers and friendship societies is to encourage a public attitude of sympathy or tolerance toward local Communist activities and the international Communist movement. Like the regular fronts, they attempt to influence the leaders of social sectors that are active partisans of change. To this end they circulate a tremendous volume of Communist-bloc propaganda literature purporting to show the "peaceful" nature and the cultural, scientific, and technological advances of the so-called "Socialist" states. They also promote visits to Latin America by cultural and other groups from Communist nations, distribute fellowships to Latin American students desiring technical or university training in Communist-bloc schools, and—in cooperation with regular fronts and mass organizations affiliated with international Communist-front groups— arrange each year for travel of Latin Americans to Communist countries. In recent years they have relied heavily on this latter device, providing low-cost or expense-free trips to the Sino-Soviet bloc for increasing numbers of politicians, intellectuals, professionals, newsmen, women, students, and labor leaders. The great majority of these are noncommunists who include a tour of the bloc enroute to or from international Communist front meetings abroad. Not all the travelers return filled with enthusiasm for the "Socialist" nations, but invariably many of them are willing to praise the Communist system, thereby enhancing the prestige of the Communist bloc and the respectability of the local Communist party.

In their efforts to generate a favorable climate of opinion the Latin American Communist parties also attempt to place secret agents in institutions which influence public and official attitudes. Primary targets are the mass-communications media, the government bureaucracy, the educational system, and other political parties. Every country in Latin America has at least a few hidden Communists in these sectors. Invariably they pose as patriotic nationalists, and frequently their true political affiliation is known only to a handful of Communist party leaders. The func-

tion of the Communist agents is to obtain strategic posts from
which they can help to determine government policies and influence popular views toward the local Communists and toward
relations with the Communist bloc and the United States. Such
hidden Communists do not ordinarily participate in the usual
party activities, for their effectiveness depends upon their ability
to present current Communist objectives without revealing their
ties with the party. The crypto-Communists do not lose their
positions if the party is repressed, and they are an invaluable
asset when it regains legal status. When the proscription against
the Chilean party was lifted in 1958, for example, five congressmen identified themselves as Communists. The existence of a
corps of crypto-Communists within the bureaucracy, the news
services, the labor movement, and various political factions facilitated the spectacular rise of the Cuban party after the fall of the
Batista regime in 1959.

The strategy and tactics employed by the Latin American
Communists over most of the past four decades have been remarkably consistent in reflecting the party's dependence on
support from other political forces. Dramatic shifts in Soviet and
Latin American Communist views of the proper relationship between the party and potential allies have resulted in some equally
dramatic changes in strategy and apparently inconsistent reversals in tactics. These, however, have nearly all been based on the
premise that the party is incapable of achieving its objectives by
its own efforts. Communist leaders, even when refusing to acknowledge the party's limitations, have always been acutely aware
of its numerical weakness and usually seek to work with or
through stronger, more respectable groups. As a general rule the
party's strength and influence increase as it obtains the cooperation of additional parties or political groups and decline when
such cooperation is withdrawn. Under the circumstances, for
more than thirty years no Communist party in Latin America has
presumed to rely exclusively on its own resources.

A review of the major changes in Communist strategy clearly
illustrates this characteristic of the movement in Latin America.
During the early years the young parties attempted, but by and

large were unable, to secure effective political alliances. To the extent that the Communists improved their political position, they did so largely through cooperation with other minor parties. Generally, in the absence of broad public response to the appeals of communism, the traditional parties which dominated the political scene in most of the area felt no need for coalitions or understandings with the fledgling Communist organizations.

During the so-called "third period" between 1928 and 1934, the Communists deluded themselves that the day of victory was at hand and insisted that prospective allies accept Communist discipline and leadership. The party was to seek power by election or revolution, as local conditions permitted, but it was not to compromise its principles by allying with other parties. The consequences of the third-period strategy were disastrous for the communist cause. The party was isolated from the people, wracked with factionalism, and effectively excluded from national politics throughout the area.

The third period was succeeded by the Popular Front, under which the Communist objective was to promote the broadest possible anti-Fascist alliance of center and leftist parties. Overnight the Communists abandoned their policy of exclusiveness to pose as reasonable and cooperative democrats, eager to subordinate partisan ambitions to the urgent task of defeating the Nazi-Fascist threat. For the first time in several Latin American countries the Communist party attained a measure of national prominence. In Chile and Cuba, where the new strategy achieved its greatest successes, the Communists worked closely with the administration parties in alliances which survived the Russo-German *rapprochement* between August 1939 and June 1941.

Elsewhere in Latin America during the twenty-two months of the Hitler-Stalin pact the party turned on its erstwhile allies, denounced the "imperialist" war, and sought, with little success, to collaborate with the neo-Nazi parties. In the process many of the recent Communist gains were lost.

The party was rescued from its untenable position by the German invasion of Russia and by the subsequent involvement of the Latin American republics in the war against the Axis.

Communist strategy was quickly revised to encourage the unity of all political forces in support of the "democratic" war. The Communists went far beyond the limits of the Popular Front in cooperating with radicals and reactionaries, democrats and dictators. Throughout much of Latin America the Communist party reached new heights in membership and political influence during and immediately after World War II, when its contacts with other parties were more extensive than ever before.

With the onset of the cold war and the general decline in the party's fortunes in the late 1940's, the Communists found it increasingly difficult to reach satisfactory understandings with their political rivals. They now advocated the formation of Communist-directed leftist coalitions in support of "antifeudal" domestic reforms and an anti-United States foreign policy, although in practice they followed the line best calculated to preserve some freedom of operation for the party under local conditions. In some countries they entered *ad hoc* electoral alliances with all parties that would accept them; in others they gave quiet "critical support" to avowedly anticommunist dictatorships.

Since the mid-1950's the Communists have returned to a modified popular-front strategy. Without abandoning their opportunistic tactics, they are seeking to cooperate as equals with all center and leftist "progressive" parties in a "democratic front of national liberation." The success of the Cuban party in exploiting the Castro revolution has led Communists in other parts of Latin America to adopt a somewhat more assertive attitude, but they continue to emphasize the need for a multiparty front.

In their public pronouncements the Communists have usually stressed the intention to gain their objectives by peaceful, constitutional means, and at times they have specifically rejected the use of force as a political weapon. Yet, since the 1920's they have been involved in revolutionary adventures in practically every country of Latin America. Once the decision has been taken to resort to force, the party has almost invariably been content to attach itself to revolutions launched by other political groups. On occasion, Latin American Communists have misinterpreted or ignored Soviet desires and have been roundly denounced by international leaders for participation in abortive revolts. In most cases, however, as in Colombia since 1948, in Cuba in the last days of the Batista regime, and in Venezuela in the early 1960's, Communist involvement in revolutionary activities has been undertaken as a calculated risk with at least tacit Soviet approval. Only twice in the history of the movement have local Communist parties played the major role in organizing and directing serious attempts to overthrow Latin American governments. Both efforts occurred in the 1930's, and both were miserable failures.

Early in 1932 the diminutive Republic of El Salvador was the scene of the first serious Communist attempt to seize power by force in the Western Hemisphere. The revolt, which lasted only a few days, was one of the bloodiest in the history of Latin America and may have cost as many as twenty-five thousand lives. At that time the Communists, the government, and most foreign observers attributed the uprising to the Communist party. This judgment gave the Communists far more credit than they deserved, but it was clear that they had ignited the spark of revolution. Repercussions within the Communist movement were catastrophic not only in El Salvador, but also in neighboring Guatemala and Honduras. Communists were executed, jailed, or exiled, and the three parties were virtually extinguished for several years.

The actions of the Salvadoran Communists, which appear in retrospect to have been irrational, were a logical outgrowth of the third-period Comintern line. The parties were urged to lead proletarian uprisings, but they were specifically prohibited from cooperating with "reformists" in such endeavors. Thus, while traditional governments in Latin America toppled like ten pins before the onslaught of real or alleged "reformist" movements during the early years of the Depression, the Communists in most countries sat on the sidelines and watched the lower classes respond to noncommunist appeals. In El Salvador, however, the position of the Communist party was unique. While popular pressures for change were high, there were no serious rivals challenging the Communist appeal to the urban proletariat and the landless peasantry. To the limited extent that these groups were organized and politically inspired, they were organized and inspired by Communists. The party, moreover, had begun to penetrate the army rank and file, whose pay was badly in arrears. In the view of Communist party leaders, all of the ingredients for a successful revolution were present.

The political situation that gave rise to the revolt in El Salvador developed rapidly in the first few days of January 1932. President Maximiliano Hernández Martínez, who had taken power after a military coup only the month before, permitted the Communist party to participate openly in municipal elections on January 5, but three days later denied it any of the seats it claimed to have won. Faced with the prospect of a quick return to clandestine status and political obscurity, the party leaders resolved to use force. On January 9 they created a revolutionary committee, appointed "Red Commanders" in various zones of the country, and called for a joint military-peasant uprising throughout the republic on January 22. They summoned Communists from Guatemala and Honduras to assist them and promised that once victory had been won in El Salvador they would spread the movement to the rest of Central America. One of their communications fell into the hands of General Ubico, dictator-president of Guatemala, who informed Salvadoran authorities. On January 18 a state of siege was declared, leading Communists were jailed, and the movement was deprived of coordination. Some rebel units received orders to cancel the revolt; others did not. Most of the would-be rebels within the army were arrested. As a result, the uprising was confined largely to the western part of the country and was conducted almost exclusively by poorly armed peasants who assumed that the entire nation was in revolt. In the absence of military discipline, the peasants gave full vent to their emotions, looting, burning, and killing hundreds of landowners and merchants. While only a small segment of the rebels were Communists, the government labeled them all as such and put down the revolt mercilessly, matching terror with terror. Communist party members were hunted down like animals. A handful who managed to escape into Guatemala were promptly jailed, to remain in prison until Ubico was overthrown twelve years later.

The second Communist-inspired revolt in Latin America occurred in Brazil in November 1935. It was both more complex in origin and more limited in execution than the Salvadoran uprising. The Brazilian revolt, which took place at a moment when the international Communist line was changing, combined some elements of third-period strategy with aspects of the Popular Front. It was actually planned and directed by local Communists and Comintern agents but was designed to appear as a united effort by all opposition forces.

The Brazilian party, which had refused to participate in the revolutions of 1930 and 1932, began laying the groundwork for the 1935 revolt more than a year before the outbreak of armed violence. Early in 1934 it launched an intensive campaign to exploit the widespread grievances of the Depression era, concentrating particularly on penetration of labor unions, peasant leagues, and the enlisted ranks of the armed forces. Popular unrest and Communist fortunes soared. In June of that year the Brazilian party formally adopted the line then known as the "united national front." Henceforth it called openly for unity of all "anti-imperialist, anti-Fascist" groups in a program to establish a national revolutionary government. This campaign resulted in March 1935 in the formation of the National Liberation Alliance, which soon claimed over one million members, of whom possibly ten thousand were Communists. The bulk of the membership was drawn from leftist and liberal parties, organized labor, the professions, the peasantry, and the military services. Overt Communist agitation and propaganda were greatly curtailed, as the party channeled most of its activities through the new front.

The Communist revolt in Brazil is identified with Luiz Carlos Prestes, who returned from the Soviet Union in April 1935 and was immediately acclaimed honorary President of the National Liberation Alliance. He was widely known as a popular hero and only incidentally as a Communist. Few Brazilians then realized that he was a member of the Executive Committee of the Comintern and the *de facto* head of the Communist movement in Brazil. Under Prestes' leadership the Alliance called for repudiation of foreign debts, expropriation of foreign holdings in Brazil, nationalization of public utilities and "imperialist" enterprises, and confiscation without compensation of all large landholdings. The activities of the Alliance were tolerated by the Vargas regime as long as there was no open call for violence, but in July 1935, when Prestes demanded "all power to the National Liberation Alliance," the movement was quickly outlawed. Its membership immediately began to dwindle.

The Communists throughout the front organization now worked feverishly to perfect their plans to overthrow the government by force, for Vargas' action had eliminated any faint possibility that the National Liberation Alliance might come to power by peaceful means. They were advised by four Comintern agents who had accompanied Prestes to Brazil. These were the German Arthur Ernst Ewert, known in Brazil as Harry Berger; the American Victor Allan Baron; the Belgian Leon Jules Vallée; and the Argentine Communist Rodolfo Ghioldi. The final plan called for simultaneous barracks revolts in widely scattered parts of the country to neutralize the armed forces and to signal a popular uprising in which the Communists were to seize power in the name of the National Liberation Alliance.

The revolt began prematurely in the northern cities of Natal and Recife in the early hours of November 24, 1935, and ended with the uprising of army aviation cadets and an infantry regiment in Rio de Janeiro three days later. The first of these was quelled in four days, the others in a matter of hours. Elsewhere in Brazil the expected insurrection failed to materialize because of lack of coordination, the continued loyalty of most of the military to the regime, and the general apathy of the civilian population. The actual fighting and casualties were confined overwhelmingly to army units. As a result of the abortive revolution the National Liberation Alliance was destroyed; Prestes, the foreign Communists, and many local party leaders were jailed for long terms; and the Communist party was reduced to impotence for another decade.

Even before the outbreak of the revolt in Brazil the Communists in Chile had begun the first serious attempt in Latin

America to achieve their objectives by parliamentary means. Under the direction of the Peruvian Eudocio Ravines, who was sent by the Comintern to Chile early in 1935, the party adopted the new policy of the Popular Front. The Chilean Communists abandoned their attitude of open hostility toward the "bourgeois" parties and sought particularly to reach an accommodation with the large Radical party. The major Socialist factions, the dissident Communists, and the small Democratic party had already formed a Left bloc when they were joined in March 1936 by the Radicals, Communists, and the Communist-led labor federation to create the formal Popular Front, which survived until 1941. Communist cooperation with the noncommunist Left was extended to the labor field as well, with the merger of separate Communist and Socialist labor organizations into the Confederation of Chilean Workers late in 1936. This change was a tactical maneuver and did not indicate any lessening of Communist efforts to win a dominant position in the trade-union movement. The Popular Front proved to be the largest political bloc in the congressional elections of 1937, when it won ten seats in the Senate and sixty-six in the Chamber of Deputies. One senator and seven deputies were Communists. The following year the Communists were instrumental in breaking a deadlock between Socialists and Radicals over the Popular Front candidate in the presidenial elections. They threw their support to Pedro Aguirre Cerda, who won office by a narrow margin in October. They then confounded their opponents by declining to accept seats in his government. This action left the Communist party comfortably free to criticize the regime at will while claiming credit for its achievements.

With the signing of the Hitler-Stalin pact and the outbreak of war in Western Europe the Communists became openly critical of their "anti-Fascist" political partners, but the latter were reluctant to jeopardize the existence of the Popular Front. The Socialists, who were seriously affected by steady Communist gains in the labor movement, finally withdrew from the administration in January 1941, after failing to have the Communists expelled from the Popular Front. The Front was then formally disbanded, although the left-wing parties continued to cooperate with the regime on an *ad hoc* basis. The effectiveness of Communist tactics was clearly demonstrated in the congressional elections of March 1941, when the party polled some 55,000 votes—more than three times its previous high—to elect three additional senators and a total of fourteen congressmen.

The Chilean Communists again became avid advocates of political cooperation among the "democratic" parties when the Soviet Union entered the war. They played a prominent role in bringing the Socialists back into the left-wing coalition, which took the name Democratic Alliance after the death of Aguirre Cerda in November 1941. During the war years the Communists once more submerged their rivalry with the Socialists but continued to exploit factionalism within the Socialist party to their own advantage. The Communist party grew steadily in numbers and influence.

Communist fortunes reached their highest point following the presidential elections of September 1946, which brought Gabriel González Videla to office at the head of a Radical-Liberal-Communist coalition. Three Communists were included in the nine-member cabinet. These were Secretary-General Carlos Contreras Labarca as Minister of Communications and Public Works, Miguel Concha as Minister of Agriculture, and Victor Contreras as Minister of Lands and Colonization. The party attempted, with considerable success, to use these positions to expand its influence throughout the country, but it tried to move too far too quickly. The other parties in the coalition became alarmed and the Cabinet fell in April 1947. The Communist ministers had served for only five months, but during that time the party had risen to 50,000 members and it had attained a dominant position in the labor movement.

Once again in the opposition, the party's position began to erode as much of its popular following melted away. With the passage of the Law for the Defense of Democracy in September 1948, outlawing the party and striking some forty thousand registered Communist voters off the electoral lists, the party was reduced to a minor irritant on the political scene. The Communists were rescued from this situation in 1952 by a new agreement with a major Socialist faction. The so-called People's Front established at that time served as the core around which the former partners of the Popular Front have regrouped in the coalition known since the mid-1950's as the Popular Action Front. Thus, the Chilean Communists attribute their resurgence to participation in a broad left-wing coalition and have been hesitant to risk a setback by engaging in political violence.

The experience of the Chilean party was repeated to a lesser degree in several parties in Latin America after the mid-1930's. While retaining the theoretical concept of the inevitability of the proletarian revolution, under the popular-front and wartime policies of cooperation the Communists counseled against political violence and were largely excluded from movements that toppled several traditional dictatorships before 1948.[1] From the beginning of the cold war until the death of Stalin in 1953, they again advocated the forceful replacement of "feudal-bourgeois dictatorships in the service of imperialism" by "democratic governments of the people"; but even in Colombia and Bolivia, where they participated in revolutionary activities during those years, the Communist appeal met with public indifference. For more than two decades after the failure of the Brazilian revolt, no Communist party played a major role in efforts to overthrow a Latin American government.

Since the mid-1950's the Communists have been obliged to adapt their tactics and strategy on the use of force to conflicting influences from international Communist sources and to changing conditions within Latin America. They have officially espoused the new doctrine of "peaceful roads to socialism," whereby a "democratic front of national liberation" might come to power by parliamentary means. At the same time noncommunist leftists have been increasingly prone to cooperate with Communists in using violence to achieve political ends, as in Venezuela in 1958,

---

1. An important exception occurred in Ecuador, where the Communist party took part in the revolution that overthrew President Arroyo del Río in May 1944. A Communist was included in the interim governing junta, which shortly transferred power to President Velasco Ibarra, who accepted Communist support for his regime.

while the Chinese Communists, later joined by the Cubans, have advocated guerrilla warfare as the appropriate device for placing Communists in or near the seats of power. Under the circumstances, although each party continues to call for a peaceful solution to the country's ills, none rules out the possibility of revolution by a coalition of Communists and other "progressive" elements. Within limits, each Latin American party is permitted to determine whether a violent or nonviolent policy or a combination of the two is most likely to achieve its objectives.

III.

The Role of the Soviet Union

Soviet Relations with the Communist Parties

THE LATIN AMERICAN COMMUNIST PARTIES HAVE NEVER BEEN FREE agents. From the beginning they have served willingly as regional branches of the international Communist movement directed from the Soviet Union. The first Communist parties in the area openly proclaimed themselves to be sections of the Communist International, and as additional parties appeared each sought formal affiliation with the Comintern. The dissolution of this body in 1943 eliminated the direct organizational link between Latin American Communists and the international movement but did not reduce their dependence upon and subservience to the Soviet state and party. The strategy and tactics pursued by the parties in Latin America have always conformed to current Soviet foreign policies, and those occasional conflicts between Soviet and Latin American party interests have invariably been resolved in favor of the Soviet Union. This prolonged close identification with an alien power and political system has been at once a major limiting factor and the most important source of strength of the Communist movement in Latin America. Except during the wartime era of good feeling between the Soviet Union and the West, the Communists' foreign ties have usually restricted their appeal to a small segment of the population. At the same time, however, the support and guidance received from abroad have provided continuity and a sense of mission without which the feeble Latin American Communist parties would long since have disappeared.

Soviet relations with the Latin American Communist parties date from the founding of the Comintern in 1919. The initiative for the first contacts came primarily from Latin Americans, inspired by what they had heard and read about the revolutionary experiment in Russia. For several years contact between the world Communist movement and its Latin American outlets was confined largely to the exchange of correspondence and to the attendance of Latin American Communists at international meetings in the Soviet Union. Although Michael Borodin visited Mexico as an agent of the Soviet regime in 1919, another three years passed before the Comintern sent non-Latin American agents into the area. On the other hand, the Argentine party—the only one then in existence in Latin America—was represented by proxy at the First Comintern Congress, while subsequent meetings of this and other international Communist bodies were usually attended by delegates from a majority of the young parties and emerging Communist groups in Latin America. Thus, it was chiefly Latin Americans who first pointed out to Communist leaders in Moscow the opportunities for the spread of communism in the region. It was largely on their own initiative that channels of communication were opened with Moscow by radical groups in several Latin American countries before the mid-1920's.

These early contacts, even though limited and largely unilateral, were vital in shaping the Communist movement in Latin America. Except for the famous "Twenty-one Conditions," by which Lenin in 1920 established the minimum standards for Communist parties everywhere, Soviet leaders did not initially force their views on the young Latin American parties. This was not necessary. From the outset these parties looked to Moscow as the Communist mecca and regarded the head of the Communist Party of the Soviet Union as the only orthodox interpreter of Marxist doctrine. Well before the struggle for Soviet leadership broke into the open in the late 1920's, the Latin American parties had adopted the custom of parroting the line of the dominant faction in the Soviet Union. It was an ingrained habit before it became compulsory for Latin American Communists to look upon the Soviet-dominated Comintern as the final arbiter in ideological and other disputes within their organizations. This process was completed when Joseph Stalin imposed his will on the international Communist movement. After 1929 those individuals unwilling to accept decisions reached in Moscow were purged, and the Latin American parties lost all semblance of independent existence.

The Comintern was the principal agency through which practical and ideological guidance was provided to the parties in Latin America. This organization, which served as the central coordinating body for communist parties throughout the world, paid little attention to Latin America during the first few years. It was presided over by Russians and Europeans who were primarily concerned with Soviet problems and the prospects for communist expansion in "capitalist" nations and their colonies. These Comintern officials long continued to regard Latin America simply as another "colonial" area and to prescribe the same tactics recommended for parties in China, India, and other dependent countries of Asia and Africa. This attitude was occasionally protested, sometimes vociferously, by Latin American Communists, who maintained that many of the problems of their area were *sui generis*. Such protests were largely ineffectual, however. As late as 1928, at the Sixth Comintern Congress, a lengthy consideration of the Latin American situation was included in a discussion of "the revolutionary movement in the colonies."

Although the leaders of the Comintern never gave Latin America a high priority, their interest in the region gradually increased with the rise in the number of Communist parties. By 1922 Alfred Stirner, a Swiss, had been placed in charge of Latin American affairs at Comintern headquarters. A special Latin American Secretariat was created within the Comintern in 1925. It appears to have been under the direction of another Swiss, Jules Humbert-Droz, while the chief Latin American member was Victorio Codovilla of Argentina. Three years later the Latin American Secretariat was enlarged to include a Caribbean Bureau and a South American Bureau, each with headquarters in the Western Hemisphere. The former, located in New York, was largely in the hands of the Communist Party of the United

States. The South American Bureau was located in Buenos Aires until 1930, when it was transferred to Montevideo. It was directed by a Lithuanian Communist, whose principal lieutenants included a Czech, a Russian, two Italians, a Tunisian, and Codovilla as treasurer. The major functions of the regional bureaus were to encourage the creation of Communist parties where they did not already exist, to support and coordinate the activities of established parties, and to serve in effect as courts of first instance in disputes arising within the Latin American Communist movement.

The establishment of the regional bureaus supplemented but did not entirely replace the previous Comintern practice of using individual agents to organize and advise the new Communist parties in Latin America. In the beginning the leadership in Moscow took advantage of the fortuitous presence of foreign radicals in Latin America for this purpose. The Russian Communist Borodin, who appears to have been sent to Mexico primarily to generate difficulties for the United States, encouraged the Indian nationalist M. N. Roy to form a Communist party and seek Comintern blessing. Roy was not a Communist at that time, nor had his presence in Mexico been arranged by the Comintern. After Roy's departure, Charles Phillips and later Bertram Wolfe were accepted by Moscow as spokesmen for the Mexican party, although neither had been sent to Mexico to serve in this capacity. In South America the Comintern apparently authorized Argentine party leaders to act as its agents in the formation of the Communist parties of Uruguay and Chile. The first international Communist agents sent into the area to carry out specific tasks assigned by the Comintern were a Japanese, Sen Katayama, and an Italian-American, Luis Fraina. In 1922 they visited the Mexican party, which they advised on both doctrine and tactics. Katayama appears to have traveled also to Central America and to have urged the Mexican Communists to assist in founding a Communist party in that area.

By the mid-1920's two types of Comintern agents were operating in Latin America. One was the temporary visitor dispatched as a trouble-shooter to resolve factional disputes or to prepare the local party leadership for a significant shift in the international Communist line. Perhaps the outstanding man in this category was Jules Humbert-Droz, who traveled widely in Brazil and parts of Spanish America in 1928. His purpose was to arrange for the Latin American Communist conferences in Montevideo and Buenos Aires the following year. These conferences thoroughly reviewed regional Communist problems in terms of the then-new "third period" Comintern line. The other type of agent was the adviser who resided indefinitely in Latin America, often becoming an official or member of the local Communist party. Among these was Alfred Stirner, who was an officer in the Mexican party and probably also a representative of the Caribbean Bureau in the late 1920's. One of Stirner's contemporaries in the Mexican Communist movement was an Italian, Vittorio Vidale, known in Latin America as Carlos Contreras, who had also served in Argentina. The Pole, who used the name Abraham or Fabio Grobart, may have been the least obtrusive of the Comintern agents. He went to Cuba in 1927 to organize the Communist underground and spent much of the next two decades as an adviser to the party there.

Even after the creation of the regional bureaus, Comintern agents continued to be sent to Latin America. Luiz Carlos Prestes was accompanied by an Argentine and three non-Latin American advisers when he returned to Brazil to launch his revolutionary adventure in 1935. In that same year the Comintern initiated its popular-front line in Chile by sending Peruvian Eudocio Ravines to Santiago at the head of a group which included a Czech, a German, an Italian, a Russian, and the Venezuelan Ricardo Martínez. More than fifteen years after the founding of the Comintern Soviet leaders evidently still regarded the Latin American Communists as too unreliable to be left entirely to their own devices and not sufficiently important to merit the personal attentions of the top leadership of the international movement.

Although the Comintern was clearly the most important of the international Communist organizations, the Latin American Communists were never obliged to rely exclusively on this agency in their relations with Moscow. Nearly all the international organizations and front groups with headquarters in the Soviet capital extended their operations to create youth wings and to affiliate these with the Communist Youth International. While few of the parties succeeded in building impressive youth auxiliaries before World War II, virtually all of them maintained at least a small youth front which dutifully affiliated with the Communist Youth International and sent delegates to the frequent meetings of the world organization in the Soviet Union. Similarly, the Latin American parties responded in the 1920's to Comintern directives that they establish local branches of the Anti-Imperialist League. This was the principal international front through which Communist parties sought to excite and direct widespread nationalistic sentiment in colonial areas. In Latin America, where national affiliates of the League were established in some countries prior to the formation of a Communist party, the chief "imperialist" target was the United States. Another important front organization with outlets in Latin America was the International Red Aid, a Communist agency employed primarily as a device for raising funds to provide legal counsel for party members and other radicals jailed by "reactionary" regimes. Every Latin American Communist party created a branch of the International Red Aid. In El Salvador the party itself operated largely through the national branch of this international front. Most of the instructions issued by party leaders for the Communist-led revolt in 1932 were sent in the name of the front organization rather than in the name of the Communist party. Elsewhere identification of the party and the front may have been somewhat less complete, but throughout Latin America the top offices in the local party, the Anti-Imperialist League, and the International Red Aid were usually held by the same small group of dedicated Communists.

Among the first of the international Communist organizations to operate in Latin America was the Red International of Labor Unions (Profintern), with which all local, regional, and national Communist-led labor organizations were expected to affiliate. As an ostensibly nonpolitical agency, its requirements for membership were less rigid than those of the Comintern. On occasion, as in Chile in 1921 and in Bolivia later in the decade, Communist groups joined the Profintern before a Communist party had been formed in the country, and in several instances its affiliates were operative before the local party was accepted as a full member of the Comintern. Nevertheless, since the Latin American Communists generally failed to make striking gains in the labor field during the 1920's, the Profintern initially attracted few important affiliates in the area. In part this situation arose also because the Red International of Labor Unions, like the Comintern, devoted most of its energies to the more promising, industrialized regions of the world, relegating Latin America to a secondary or tertiary position. A further difficulty was caused by the lack of a "uniform line on the trade-union question" by the Profintern and Comintern, which was openly criticized by at least one Latin American delegate at the Sixth Comintern Congress in 1928.

These problems were partially resolved by the convening of the Latin American Communist labor conference in Montevideo in May 1929. The need for such a conference had first been expressed formally by Latin American delegates to a Profintern meeting held in connection with the tenth anniversary of the Russian Revolution late in 1927. The Montevideo conference was the first large-scale Communist meeting in Latin America and was generally interpreted by the Communists of this region as evidence that the leadership in Moscow had finally recognized their potential. It was attended by representatives of the Profintern, the Comintern, the major international front organizations, and the Communist-dominated French labor confederation as well as by Communist and procommunist labor leaders from fifteen Latin American republics. Its chief accomplishment was the creation of the Latin American Trade Union Confederation as an affiliate of the Profintern, which now accepted a Latin American on its Executive Committee. The Confederation soon claimed to represent national labor organizations from ten Latin American countries and groups of trade unions from seven others—all except the Dominican Republic, Haiti, and Nicaragua. A few of these labor bodies, such as those from Cuba and

Chile, were truly national in scope, but the majority were paper organizations or small Communist fractions which had recently split off from noncommunist labor federations in response to third-period directives. At this time Communists unable to seize or maintain control of existing labor unions or federations were instructed to create competing organizations in order to preserve complete independence from "reformist" elements. The Latin American Trade Union Confederation probably reached its peak in 1930 and thereafter quickly lost strength with the general decline of Communist fortunes in the area. It survived, however, until 1935, when the Communist International adopted the popular-front line and Communists were again encouraged to cooperate with other political groups in the labor movement. Meanwhile it had performed a highly useful function, serving as the Profintern's regional agency for dispensing funds, teaching organizational techniques, and providing another point of contact between the Latin American parties and the Soviet Union.

At least one official Soviet-government organization appears to have served as a link between the Latin American Communists and Moscow in the decade ending in 1935. This was the Soviet Trading Corporation, which maintained an office in New York and two offices, under the name Iumtorg, in the River Plate area. Iumtorg's director, Boris Kraevsky, opened the first office in Montevideo in 1925 and the second one in Buenos Aires the following year. He is credited with persuading the Uruguayan government to extend formal diplomatic recognition to the Soviet Union in 1926, and in 1930 was appointed his country's "general representative" to Uruguay. In the meantime Kraevsky made his headquarters in Buenos Aires, but traveled widely in Brazil and southern South America, ostensibly in connection with his commercial activities. Although the evidence is incomplete, it is probable that Kraevsky's principal function was to supply the Communist parties with propaganda and funds. His position as regional director of Iumtorg was an excellent cover for this role. In any event, within a few years authorities in several South American republics were convinced that the Iumtorg director and his associates were engaged in subversive activities, inciting

Communist riots in Uruguay and Argentina and attempting to foment violence in southern Brazil and Paraguay. By the early 1930's Kraevsky's usefulness as a Soviet agent was greatly diminished. He was denied entry into Brazil in 1930. In Argentina the Uriburu regime closed Iumtorg's Buenos Aires office in mid-1931, arresting the 160 employees. Kraevsky himself was deported from Chile by the revolutionary junta which seized power in June 1932. The South American Communists, however, continued to obtain propaganda and other support from Montevideo until 1935, when Uruguay severed relations with the Soviet Union and Iumtorg's operations came to an end.

It is evident that the young Communist parties of Latin America must have received substantial financial assistance from the international movement. Almost from the beginning the relative affluence of the Communists was a cause for comment by other political groups in Latin America, for the small parties maintained newspapers, engaged in costly political and propaganda campaigns, and conducted other overt activities obviously beyond their local resources. A large part of their expenses was underwritten ultimately by the Soviet Union, although the funds were distributed through a wide variety of channels. The Comintern appears to have been the principal immediate source of assistance for many years, and its regional bureaus were established in part to dispense regular subventions to some of the parties. Such subsidies varied according to the importance of the party and to the opportunities of the moment. Robert Alexander notes that the Chilean party, which had been receiving $1,800 monthly from the Comintern, was given $10,000 in June 1932 when its prospects momentarily brightened. The travel of Latin American delegates to international meetings was usually paid by the host organization, and on occasion the delegates were authorized to convey funds to their own and neighboring parties on their return. Traveling Comintern agents also often served in this capacity. Luis Fraina, of the Communist Party of the United States, was reported to have given several thousand dollars to the Mexican party for a political campaign in 1922, and the agent known as Franz Gruber, who had been charged with the task of reviving the shattered Brazilian party, received about $40,000 for this purpose from Communist sources in the United States before his arrest in Brazil in 1939. In connection with the Brazilian Communist uprising in November 1935, the Soviet Union was alleged to have transmitted funds through its diplomatic and commercial agencies in Montevideo. It was reported that the Soviet legation and the Iumtorg office had been allocated $100,000 to promote revolts in Brazil and Argentina and that an unusually large amount of Soviet gasoline had been sold for local currency in Brazil prior to the revolt in order to make additional funds available to the Brazilian party. Since World War II, with the creation of the Soviet bloc and the considerable expansion in the number of Soviet and satellite diplomatic missions in the area, the use of diplomatic posts for distribution of Soviet financial support to the Latin American Communist parties has increased substantially.

With the shift to the popular-front line, which was confirmed by the Seventh Comintern Congress in August 1935, most of the original international Communist organizations disappeared in response to instructions from the Soviet Union. These had become a liability for they were clearly identified as hostile toward Socialists and other "reformists" with whom the Communists were now urged to cooperate. Thus, the Profintern and its Latin American affiliates, for example, were disbanded and Communists en masse entered the stronger labor bodies they had previously opposed. The established international front groups also were dropped, but these were quickly replaced by a galaxy of new organizations designed to appeal to the sympathies of liberals and the democratic left. While the Latin American Communists continued until the war years to denounce "Yankee imperialism" in the hemisphere, they reflected the more immediate concern of the Soviet Union over the spread of fascism in Europe and Asia. Therefore, most of the new fronts which were introduced throughout Latin America featured such themes as "pro-democracy," "pro-peace," "anti-fascism," and friendship for the peoples of China and Spain. On the whole, Soviet direction of the new front organizations was well disguised. At least partially for this reason the new fronts were generally more successful than their predecessors in attracting noncommunist support.

For more than a decade after the Seventh Comintern Congress there were no comparable international meetings to attract large numbers of Latin American delegates to the Soviet Union simultaneously. Until 1941 and again after the war, direct contact between the Soviet and Latin American parties was maintained through visits of individual Communists to the Soviet capital and by the continued travel of Comintern agents to Latin America. The current propaganda line was transmitted on occasion through such travelers, but it was sent more regularly through the international Communist press and the Communist parties of Western Europe and the United States. By the late 1930's some propaganda guidance was also being sent from Moscow to the Latin American Communist parties by short-wave radio. During these years the international Communist bureaucracy in the Soviet Union provided a haven for a substantial number of Latin American Communist exiles, such as the Brazilian Octavio Brandão, who broadcast regularly in Portuguese to Brazil from about 1938 until the end of the second world war.

Normal relations between the Soviet and Latin American parties were seriously disrupted for more than four years following the German invasion of Russia in June 1941. Except for occasional coordination efforts by the Communist Party of the United States, the Latin American Communists at this time were left largely to their own devices to determine the precise strategy and tactics to apply to the local situation. Under the circumstances it is significant that none of them took advantage of Soviet weakness to strike out on an independent line, even after Stalin dissolved the Comintern in May 1943, thus theoretically severing their remaining links with Moscow. Every Latin American Communist leader regarded the threat to the Soviet Union as a direct threat to the local party and subordinated all other objectives to preservation of the Soviet state. Taking their cue from Stalin's wartime pronouncements—which were now carried by the noncommunist wire services—the Communists exerted their full efforts to promote political harmony and maximum production of war materials, while portraying the Soviet Union and the international movement as respectable, democratic, and nonrevolutionary. The conduct of the Latin American Communist parties during the war years proved beyond question their complete and voluntary identification with the Soviet cause and their ability to serve as effective spokesmen for that cause in the absence of frequent contact with the leaders of international communism.

The close of World War II initiated a new phase in the international Communist movement, for the Soviet Union was no longer the only Communist nation. By 1948 seven Central European states—Poland, East Germany, Czechoslovakia, Hungary, Rumania, Bulgaria, and Albania—had become satellites of the Soviet Union, and Yugoslavia had also fallen under Communist domination. In this situation the Soviet Union did not seek or desire to revive the prewar system whereby its direction of the outlying parties had been exercised through the Comintern and other agencies with headquarters in Moscow. While Soviet leaders moved quickly to reassert their control over the world Communist movement, a serious effort was made to preserve the illusion of autonomy among the parties of Latin America and elsewhere. For this purpose a whole new network of front organizations and a new coordinating agency were established with central offices outside the Soviet Union. Through this apparatus Soviet guidance of the Latin American and other Communist parties was less direct, but no less real than before.

Six of the postwar Communist-front organizations came into existence within a year after the close of hostilities. These were the World Federation of Trade Unions, founded in October 1945; the International Federation of Democratic Women and the World Federation of Democratic Youth, both created in November 1945; the International Union of Students, which was formed in Prague at the first World Congress of Students, in 1946; the International Association of Democratic Jurists; and the World Federation of Teachers' Unions. Both of the latter were founded in 1946. Except for the student front, all these organizations originally had headquarters in Paris. The front organizations were born of the spirit of international cooperation and good will between East and West that gave rise to the United Nations. For this reason they differed initially from the traditional Communist fronts in being more truly democratic and representative of various shades of opinion than had been customary in Communist-penetrated institutions. This distinction, however, was soon lost as the new fronts came increasingly under Communist control and were converted into vehicles for disseminating the Soviet propaganda line. By 1949 their Communist character had become so obvious that most noncommunist affiliates withdrew to form competing international bodies. At about the same time the Communist fronts began seeking more congenial surroundings, with all except the lawyers' association eventually transferring their headquarters to Soviet-satellite countries.

From the beginning the postwar network of front organizations was extended to Latin America, and new affiliates joined as the Communists created additional local and national fronts or gained the leadership of previously noncommunist associations. By the time the true nature of the international fronts became apparent in the late 1940's, Communist control of the women's, youths', teachers', and lawyers' affiliates was sufficiently strong to prevent any significant defections. In the case of the International Union of Students, there was no mass withdrawal of Latin American members. Rather, university-student organizations tended to act individually, affiliating when they were under Communist leadership and withdrawing when noncommunists gained control of the local student body. Thus, the number of member organizations in the area has fluctuated widely, serving in effect as a barometer of Communist fortunes in the Latin American student movement. With respect to the labor front, noncommunist affiliates generally transferred allegiance to the new International Confederation of Free Trade Unions and its subsidiary, the Inter-American Regional Labor Organization. Only the Communist-dominated Confederation of Latin American Workers, the Chilean central labor confederation, and small

Communist fractions in a few other national labor bodies continued their affiliation with the World Federation of Trade Unions after 1949.

The most important of the international Communist-front organizations in the postwar period has been the World Peace Council, which was created as a propaganda instrument for use in the cold war. Every active Communist party in Latin America was instructed to form and maintain a national peace front and to stimulate popular interest in the peace movement. The peace campaign was launched in Poland in 1948 with the World Congress of Intellectuals for Peace, primarily a Communist gathering, which convoked the First World Peace Congress, held in Paris and Prague the following year. In addition to well-meaning noncommunists from many countries, prominent Communists and sympathizers from the leading Latin American nations attended this congress. The first peace congress gave rise to the World Committee of Peace Partisans, which was converted in 1950 into the World Peace Council, as it has been known since. The peace front has been more successful than most of the postwar international Communist organizations in attracting the continuing support of prominent noncommunist intellectuals from countries around the globe. Virtually all the Latin American members, however, are consistent joiners of national, regional, and international front groups. Few, if any, of them are unaware of the political orientation of the World Peace Council.

None of the international Communist-front organizations has been an unqualified success in rallying broad Latin American support for the Soviet propaganda line. With few exceptions the Latin American affiliates are small and have only a limited impact on the general populace. Yet, they have succeeded in their primary objectives, to serve as channels of communication and to influence opinion-molding sectors of society. Each of the international fronts pours tremendous quantities of prepared propaganda materials into Latin America, thereby subsidizing and directing a considerable portion of the parties' propaganda activities. Each of them includes Latin American Communists or sympathizers on its Executive Committee and staff. Each holds periodic meetings and subsidizes the travel of delegations from the various Latin American countries. These delegations are usually comprised not only of Communist party members, but also of students, politicians, labor leaders, journalists, professionals, and others currently or potentially important in national public life. Travel arrangements are invariably handled locally by Communists or by trusted sympathizers, whose influence and respectability are increased in proportion to the patronage they dispense. In the postwar period the Latin American Communists, and many noncommunists, have regularly taken advantage of international front meetings abroad to visit the Soviet Union and other countries of the Sino-Soviet bloc. Thus, the international fronts have provided ample opportunities for consultation between Latin American Communists and leaders of the international movement.

In October 1947 the Soviet leaders created a new international party agency. This was the Communist Information Bureau (Cominform), which assumed some of the coordinating functions previously exercised by the Comintern and which supplemented the front organizations as links between the Soviet Union and the distant Communist parties. In the postwar pattern it was located outside of the Soviet Union, at first in Belgrade and after 1948 in Bucharest. Its basic purpose appears to have been to publish and distribute an official international Communist newspaper, *For a Lasting Peace, For a People's Democracy!* Since the dissolution of the Comintern four years earlier, there had been no single orthodox journal available to each of the Communist parties in the local language. Latin American editions were published in Spanish and Portuguese. The Cominform press was designed primarily to provide straight information for internal party consumption. It enabled Communists throughout Latin America and elsewhere to receive, regularly and promptly, Soviet interpretations of international events and Soviet-approved versions of developments within the Communist camp. Soviet views of the Titoist heresy in Yugoslavia, for example, were fully aired in the pages of the Cominform newspaper.

Although the Cominform was initially launched as a service agency for the international movement, it soon acquired political attributes as well. It was commonly regarded by Communists and noncommunists alike as the successor to the Comintern. Like its predecessor, it maintained a large international staff, on which numerous Latin Americans served from time to time. While it was not necessary for the various Communist parties to affiliate formally with the Cominform, recognition by this body was tantamount to acceptance by the Soviet Union. In Latin America in the 1950's dissident Communist factions in Brazil, Colombia, Mexico, Peru, and Venezuela were denied recognition and service by the Cominform.

It is significant that neither the Cominform nor the elaborate network of communist-front organizations established after World War II provided for regional coordinating centers in Latin America. In the postwar years there was no equivalent of the earlier Caribbean and South American Bureaus of the Comintern. Although the larger and more active parties continued to provide assistance and counsel to the smaller Communist organizations in Latin America, each of the parties maintained its direct ties with the Soviet Union. For a time in the early 1950's, when the Communists in Guatemala were close to power, Soviet leaders apparently delegated certain regional responsibilities to the Guatemalan party. Communists from various Latin American republics were sent to that country for extended training and experience under the supervision of Guatemalan party leaders. This practice terminated abruptly with the collapse of the Arbenz regime in 1954. Subsequent sporadic attempts to set up clandestine training schools in Latin America usually failed until after the Castro revolution in Cuba.

In the course of the anti-Stalin campaign in 1956, when Soviet leaders were seeking to demonstrate the autonomous and peaceful nature of the international Communist movement, the Cominform was suddenly dissolved as the Comintern had been dissolved under comparable circumstances thirteen years earlier. Again, the sacrifice of the Communist agency was purely a tactical move. The international Communist publication reappeared in 1958, this time edited in Prague as the monthly *World Marxist Review: Problems of Peace and Socialism*. It is published simultaneously in translation in Brazil and Spanish America.

The Latin American Communists, and their counterparts around the world, were not allowed to develop any false illusions about the much-vaunted political autonomy of the parties in the postwar period. Even before the wartime spirit of cooperation between East and West had begun to cool, the Soviet Union insisted prominent party leaders abroad must issue public statements revealing that their true loyalties lay with the Soviet cause rather than with their native country. In 1946 and 1947 most of the well-known Communist leaders in Latin America were obliged to speak out in this vein. The same theme was usually incorporated in the endless panegyrics about the genius of Stalin and the Paradise-like qualities of the Soviet Union which were included as a matter of course, while Stalin lived, in both policy and propaganda statements by the Latin American parties and their chief spokesmen. A typical example of the latter was composed by the Brazilian writer Jorge Amado, in 1951. It reads in part:

> There is today no sentiment more noble in the heart of any man than love for the Soviet Union.
> Love for the Soviet Union is like a grandiose summation of all that a man can love on earth, a summation of all the great sentiments, the purest and most noble. If one loves his wife and children, his father and mother, if he possesses in his heart love for his family, the desire to see his children born happy, then he must love the U.S.S.R., where children's lives pass as in a paradise, where unsheltered and unhappy old age is unknown, where family relations are devoid of any vestige of meanness, where love for relatives can attain its full beauty. . . .
> And what does patriotism mean? I do not know how one can conceive today of a true patriot who does not at the same time love the Soviet Union with the deepest love.[1]

Since the anti-Stalin campaign, which began in February 1956, Soviet leaders have found it necessary to instruct the Latin American Communists to be less effusive in their public decla-

---

1. Jorge Amado, *O mundo da paz* (Rio de Janeiro, 1951), p. 16.

rations of loyalty and affection for the Communist motherland. There is no question, however, that as long as the Soviet Union remains the dominant Communist power, the Latin American parties will resume their fulsome praise of that country and its leaders whenever it becomes necessary or politic for them to do so.

In the last years of the Stalin era the Soviet Union increased its direct contacts with the Communist parties of Latin America and other regions. This objective was accomplished by reviving the prewar practice of summoning Communist leaders from all parts of the world to meet together periodically in Moscow. Since 1952, Communist delegations from Latin America and elsewhere have traveled to the Soviet Union more frequently and in larger numbers than ever before to attend Soviet Party Congresses and special commemorative celebrations held in the Russian capital. Such mass gatherings, designed initially to demonstrate the avowed strength and unity of the Communist camp in the cold war, have become major instruments of Soviet coordination and control over the outlying parties. Since the death of Stalin the new heads of the Soviet state and party have employed these meetings as forums for launching the anti-Stalin campaign, for issuing startling reinterpretations of Marxist-Leninist doctrine, and for countering the Chinese Communist challenge to Soviet leadership of the world Communist movement.

Attendance at the Moscow meetings has given the Latin American Communists a sense of more active participation in international Communist affairs and of greater Soviet interest in their area and problems. Their delegates not only have heard the full Soviet arguments on each ideological debate and shift in global strategy, but have also had the benefit of meeting jointly with Soviet leaders for consideration of special tactics to be employed in Latin America. At least a dozen Latin American parties sent observers to the Nineteenth Congress of the Communist Party of the Soviet Union in 1952. At that time they were advised to seek the leadership of the "national liberation" movement and to denounce publicly the "reactionary regimes in the service of imperialism." Representatives from eighteen Latin American Communist parties attended the Twentieth Soviet Party Congress in February 1956. There they felt repercussions of the new campaign against the "cult of the personality" and were instructed to modify their strategy in line with the new doctrine of "peaceful roads to socialism" and "peaceful coexistence." In November 1957 the ceremonies commemorating the fortieth anniversary of the Russian Revolution again attracted delegations from eighteen Latin American parties. A caucus of the delegates was given specific directives on the new line to be adopted in Latin America. The parties were to emphasize nationalism, to identify themselves with the legitimate aspirations of the Latin American people, and, wherever possible, to encourage noncommunists to lead the national-liberation movement. At the Twenty-first Congress of the Soviet party in 1959 Latin American observers were urged to work more closely together and to convoke their own party Congresses at more frequent intervals.

In 1960 the Latin American Communist parties were called upon to give full support to the Cuban revolution and to the Soviet Union in its dispute with Communist China. In response to Soviet directives delegations from several Latin American parties in June attended the Rumanian Party Congress, where Khrushchev presented the Soviet view of the ideological dispute, and in August fourteen of the parties sent fraternal delegations to the Eighth Congress of the party in Cuba. These demonstrations of Latin American Communist solidarity were eclipsed by the attendance of Communists from all twenty republics at the Moscow Meeting of Communist and Workers' Parties in November. It was the first time that Communists from all Latin American countries had ever met together simultaneously. This fact reflected the seriousness of the ideological conflict within the Communist camp, the increasing importance attached by the Soviet party to the Latin American Communist movement, and the continued subservience of the Latin American Communists to the demands of Moscow.

Since 1960 all of the Latin American Communist leaders have

visited the Soviet Union for individual consultation or as observers at the Twenty-second Congress of the Soviet Party in
1962. Most of them have also attended Party Congresses in one
or more of the satellite countries. Both in Moscow and in the
European Communist capitals they have been advised to avoid
a dogmatic approach to the problems of the revolution in Latin
America, adapting violent or nonviolent tactics as local circumstances dictate.

As their importance to the Soviet Union has mounted, the
Latin American parties have received an increasing flow of
material aid from international Communist sources abroad. It
was estimated, even before the Castro revolution, that the Soviet
bloc was investing the equivalent of 100 million dollars annually
in the propaganda campaign in Latin America. The bulk of this
investment is in the form of propaganda materials and services,
but a substantial portion is provided as direct financial support
to individual Communist parties. It is not possible to determine
even the approximate amount of such aid because of the secrecy
surrounding financial transactions within the Communist movement and because the Communists prefer to leave the question
unclear.

Since the dissolution of the Comintern the Soviet Union has
maintained, publicly and officially, that the outlying Communist
parties are fully autonomous, self-supporting entities, with no
ties to the international movement other than a common adherence to Marxist-Leninist doctrine. For their part the Latin American parties have also been reluctant to publicize their financial
relations with the Soviet Union and international Communist
organizations. They have been primarily concerned not to
jeopardize their position as ostensible "national" parties by
revealing the extent to which they are dependent on Soviet
subsidies. Yet, at the same time they have found it advantageous
to leave the impression that they do, indeed, receive extensive
aid from abroad. In the absence of complete or accurate information on this subject, the Latin American press and public have
long tended to exaggerate the amount of financial assistance
extended to the local Communist parties. During the popular-

front period, if not earlier, the Communist parties discovered that their presumed wealth enabled them to enlist political allies who would not otherwise have been attracted by their limited following and their local fund-raising capabilities. Thus, beyond periodic and perfunctory denials that any outside aid is received, the Communists do nothing to dispel the popular belief that they have access to unlimited funds. They have continued to exploit this advantage in their relations with other parties wherever they have enjoyed even partial freedom of operation.

The Cuban Revolution and the Sino-Soviet Dispute

THE CONVERSION OF CUBA INTO A "SOCIALIST REPUBLIC" AND THE emergence of China as a major Communist power have opened new perspectives for the Latin American Communist movement. Although the impact of these events has presented the Soviet Union with its greatest opportunity in Latin America, these developments have raised new problems in Soviet relations with the local Communist parties. The Cuban revolution and the subsequent massive Soviet aid to the Castro regime have given the Communists cause to hope for sweeping victories throughout Latin America. Even before Castro's public espousal of Marxism-Leninism, Cuba had become a highly effective regional center for Communist activities, supplementing Latin American party ties with the Soviet Union. Yet, at the same time, Castro's victory over Batista—incorrectly interpreted as the victory of dedicated guerrilla troops over a professional army—has lent credence to Chinese assertions that violence is the only practical route to power and has cast doubt on the validity for Latin America of the Khrushchev doctrine of peaceful roads to socialism. That the basic premise of this argument is erroneous has been ignored by those Communists dissatisfied with the comparatively re-strained policies advocated by the Soviet Union and implemented by Moscow-oriented party leaders. The Chinese Communists, in challenging the Soviet role as sole and infallible interpreter of Marxism-Leninism, offer their impatient Latin American com-rades a new source of leadership and a strategy that is portrayed as particularly suited to Latin American conditions. The number of Latin American Communists prepared to follow the Chinese

173

line is still insignificant, but for the first time dissident party members have an alternative to Soviet leadership within the world Communist movement.

Serious interest in the Chinese party is a recent and still limited development among Latin American Communists. For a time in the 1920's the Latin American parties reflected the Comintern line on China as a promising model for Communist expansion in a "colonial" country, but they paid only sporadic and fleeting attention to the area after the failure of the Chinese Communist bid for power in 1927. This situation persisted through the next two decades. There was no indication of direct Chinese influence on the Latin American movement during these years, although Eudocio Ravines gives the Chinese Communists credit for inspiring the popular-front tactics he introduced into Chile in the mid-1930's. Even the final victory of the Communists in China in 1949 elicited little more than *pro forma* congratulations from the Latin American Communist parties. During the Korean War, however, a few Latin American Communists visited China while on tour of the Communist camp. By the mid-1950's visits to Peking and Shanghai had become a regular feature of such tours for a growing number of Latin American Communist travelers. The rising importance of China in the international Communist movement was shown in 1960, when representatives of fifteen Latin American parties attended the ceremonies commemorating the eleventh anniversary of the Chinese Communist regime.

The small minority of Latin American Communists who visited China seems to have been drawn initially by the lure of the exotic. They were soon struck, however, by the apparent similarities between the problems of China and their own countries and by the identity of views between the Chinese and themselves toward United States "imperialism." For the most part the Latin American travelers returned home with glowing accounts of the methods and accomplishments of the Communists in overcoming China's perennial poverty and in converting the country into a powerful industrialized nation. They usually suggested that much in the experience of the Chinese party was applicable to Latin America. Representatives of the Guatemalan and Brazilian parties were particularly impressed with the importance of building a strong base among the peasant masses, although the Guatemalan Communists were quashed before they could organize a significant rural following, and the Brazilian party leaders were not convinced of the need for a mass peasant organization until after the success of the Cuban revolution.

The Chinese Communists spared no effort to make a favorable impression on the Latin American visitors, who were flattered by the hospitality and special treatment accorded by their hosts. Latin American Communists who had never seen Stalin or Malenkov or Khrushchev were received in audience by Mao Tse-tung and Foreign Minister Chou En-lai. From the first contacts, the Chinese leaders encouraged their Latin American comrades to regard the Chinese experiment with socialism as a model to be followed in Latin America. The Latin American Communists were offered both guidance and support. The full cost of the trip from the Soviet Union to China and return appears to have been paid by the Chinese government. While the bulk of the Latin American Communist travelers spent only a short time in China as tourists or as delegates to international front meetings, some of them—probably not more than a few dozen in the decade after 1952—remained for several months of intensive training in organizational techniques, ideology, and guerrilla warfare. The majority of the trainees appears to have come from the Pacific coast countries and from small Latin American parties with no prospects for gaining power except by revolution.

The Chinese Communists—like their Soviet counterparts—have sought to further both partisan and national objectives in their contacts with Latin America. Thus, their attempts to attract and influence the Latin American Communist parties have been interwoven with a campaign to gain enhanced prestige and recognition for their regime among Latin American government officials and opinion-molding sectors of the population. In conducting these parallel campaigns they have been obliged to rely heavily on the international Communist-front apparatus and its outlets in Latin America. Beginning in the mid-1950's a series of binational centers and cultural societies were organized by local Communists in several Latin American countries to facilitate travel and the exchange of propaganda with Communist China and to call attention to Spanish-language broadcasts initiated by Radio Peking in 1957. As early as 1956 noncommunist members of Latin American front groups comprised a significant percentage of all Latin Americans traveling to Communist China, and by 1959 noncommunist intellectuals, journalists, publishers, congressmen, and business and labor leaders far outnumbered Communists among the four hundred Latin American visitors to Peking. Travel to Latin America from China also began in 1956, with the tour of the large Chinese Circus which visited several of the republics. The success of this exotic novelty in attracting favorable comment encouraged Chinese leaders to send the more elaborate Peking Opera on a similar tour in Latin America in 1959–1960.

A major increase in the Chinese Communist propaganda effort in Latin America coincided with the success of the Cuban revolution. In 1959 and 1960 New China News Agency representatives toured the region, arranging an exchange agreement with the Cuban-based *Prensa Latina* news agency and engaging their own correspondents in at least four countries. At the same time the flow of printed materials from China increased sharply, to reach flood proportions in 1960. The intensified propaganda effort and the additional services provided by the Chinese were of immediate and primary benefit to the Communist parties and front groups. A significant number of noncommunist publishers also accepted the wire service, and books in Spanish on Chinese culture, the writings of Mao Tse-tung, and periodicals such as *China Reconstructs* were distributed widely through noncommunist as well as through Communist outlets. An additional instrument in the propaganda campaign was the Chinese-Latin American Friendship Association, created in Peking in March 1960 to promote increased Latin American travel and to publicize the favorable comments of visitors to the Chinese mainland.

Chinese propaganda directed toward such visitors and toward

the Latin Americans at home concentrated on two principal themes. The first of these was to portray the Chinese People's Republic as a legitimate, peace-loving, and increasingly powerful member of the community of nations. The second was to cast the United States in the role of international villain, as a war-mongering, imperialistic power bent on keeping Latin America in "colonial bondage." Communist China was presented as ready and able to assist the Latin Americans—by example and through increased trade and technological exchange—to surmount the problems of underdevelopment. This impression was strengthened somewhat by occasional Chinese purchases of Latin American surplus commodities and by the establishment of a modest student-exchange program with Chile in 1960. The first real opportunity for the Chinese Communists to demonstrate the sincerity of their intentions toward Latin America, however, came when the Castro administration, late in 1960, accepted large-scale trade and aid offers in exchange for diplomatic recognition of the Peking regime. The Cuban action, depicted as the exercise of national sovereignty in defiance of the United States, not only marked a major success in the Chinese Communists' quest for respectability, but also enhanced their appeal among ultranationalists throughout Latin America.

The Cuban revolution was a boon to the Chinese Communists, providing them excellent ammunition for both the emerging dispute with the Soviet Union and their propaganda offensive against the United States in Latin America and elsewhere. China, thus, was the first Communist power to give unstinting propaganda support to the Castro regime, extolling it almost from the outset as a glorious struggle by Latin American patriots against "Yankee imperialism." As interpreted by propagandists in Peking, Castro's success in January 1959 proved beyond question that the Chinese experience in seizing power at the head of a peasant revolution was the appropriate strategy for revolutionaries in underdeveloped areas. The Chinese also hammered incessantly on the theme that only the solidarity of Latin American nationalists and the Communist camp with Cuba would prevent the destruction of the Castro regime by the "frenzied colonialist forces in the United States." It is not possible to determine the extent of Chinese Communist influence in shaping Latin American attitudes toward the Cuban revolution. Probably it was slight. Latin Americans favorably disposed toward the new Cuban government tended independently to regard it as a protest against United States domination of the island. Nevertheless, the similarity of views between pro-Castro Latin Americans and Chinese Communists on the Cuban issue made it easier for the former to accept other Chinese propaganda statements at face value.

The early propaganda treatment of the Cuban revolution also exposed the growing divergence between Chinese Communist and Soviet counsel to the Latin American Communist parties. The Chinese praised the Castro regime for having "broken the chain of colonialism fastened on Latin America" by the United States. According to Peking, the Castro revolution demonstrated convincingly that victory over United States imperialism "can be won by waging a resolute struggle, and by no other way." The Chinese "hate America" campaign had consistently been more virulent than the Soviet line, but in 1959 and early 1960 it stood in marked contrast to the Soviet doctrine of peaceful coexistence. While the Chinese Communists were urging their Latin American comrades to use violence, the Soviet Union was seeking a *rapprochement* with the West, softening its own propaganda attacks on the United States, and advising the Latin American Communists to present themselves as progressive nationalists rather than as violent revolutionaries. Even after Mikoyan's visit to Cuba in February 1960, the Soviet Union continued to describe the Castro regime as "progressive" and to deny that it was hostile to the United States. Clearly, for those Communists who saw the Castro revolution as a model to be followed everywhere in Latin America, the Chinese line was more appealing than the initial Soviet position on Cuba.

There is reason to believe that during 1959 the Soviet Union may actually have encouraged the Chinese to pursue their more strident line on the Cuban revolution as counterpoint to the "responsible" attitude assumed publicly by the Kremlin leaders.

In any event, the existence of the two international Communist views on Cuba was a tactical advantage to the Latin American Communist parties. For well over a year after Castro seized power the Communists elsewhere in Latin America were free to adopt whichever line seemed appropriate to local circumstances and most attractive to the immediate audience they were seeking to influence. Once the Sino-Soviet dispute had hardened, however, and the question of strategy and tactics was subordinated to that of international party discipline, this freedom of choice was somewhat curtailed. The Latin American parties formally endorsed the Soviet line calling for a "peaceful transition to socialism" wherever possible. Although the use of violence was not excluded, the Latin American Communists were obliged to deny the Chinese thesis that revolution was the only practical way to achieve power.

It is significant that there is no basis in fact for the efforts by Peking—and by some Western observers—to identify Castro's victory over Batista as a Latin American example of Chinese guerrilla tactics in action. The similarities between the guerrilla-warfare methods taught by the Chinese and employed by Cubans was almost entirely coincidental, for Chinese Communist influence on the rebel movement was virtually nil. Cuban revolutionary leaders have since acknowledged that they were woefully ignorant of the writings of Mao Tse-tung on guerrilla warfare. In the fight against Batista they simply adopted the methods used by Cuban rebels in the long war against Spain in the nineteenth century. Mao's popularity among Cubans as an authority on unconventional warfare developed after Castro came to power.

The assertion that Castro's rebels consciously employed Chinese military tactics is only one of many myths about the Cuban revolution perpetuated by the Castro regime, by its friends, and by its enemies. Perhaps the most persistent and effective myth about this revolution is the one which holds that Castro and his tiny band of dedicated followers forged a peasant army which defeated the professional armed forces of Cuba on the field of battle. Castro's forces, in fact, were drawn primarily from the middle class and never approached the proportions of an army. They represented, moreover, only one of numerous, uncoordinated, and ineffectual protest groups which had taken up arms against the Batista regime. As the least exposed and least vulnerable of such groups, the guerrillas who owed allegiance to Castro were able to survive until the regime fell as the result of the hostility of the bulk of the civilian population and the almost total demoralization of the armed forces. Nevertheless, as the best-publicized and, by January 1959, the largest of the organized anti-Batista groups, Castro's 26th of July Movement was able to take power and to claim credit for overthrowing the dictatorship. From that time the image of Castro as a latter-day David scattering the hordes of Batista and driving him into exile has been seized upon throughout Latin America by would-be revolutionaries who have been encouraged to believe that they, too, can defeat the local Goliath with little more than a strong will and the backing of the peasantry.

Almost from the beginning Castro's rebel movement received support from liberal and left-of-center sources in Cuba and elsewhere in the Western Hemisphere. It appears, however, to have received no direct assistance or inspiration from any Communist source until mid-1958. Certainly, Castro received neither aid nor comfort from the Cuban Communist organization before that time. The Cuban party leaders, who had never profited from violence but had achieved their greatest success through accommodation with the government, classed Castro as a "bourgeois opportunist." His attack on Moncada Barracks in 1953 was dismissed as a "putschist" action. At that time Communist and noncommunist observers alike could see little in Castro to distinguish him from other political gangsters thrown up by the Cuban political milieu of the 1940's and 1950's. His invasion of Cuba in December 1956 was ignored almost entirely by the Communist press, and party leaders consistently rejected all opportunities to cooperate with the rebel movement. With good reason the Communist party could claim at least partial credit for the complete failure of the general strike called by Castro in April 1958.

The ability of Castro's rebel group to survive and to expand in the face of its rejection by organized labor and the brutal repression of the opposition by the regime in the spring of 1958 convinced the Communist leadership that Castro could no longer be ignored. Some party members, like other Cubans, were strongly attracted by Castro's appeal. Primarily as a matter of insurance, the party sent an emissary to the Castro camp in the late spring and detailed Carlos Rafael Rodríguez to attach himself to Castro's headquarters in June 1958. Rodríguez appears to have found that Castro had no objections to Communist support for his cause. As popular resistance to Batista and acceptance of Castro mounted during the latter months of the year, able-bodied Communists were instructed to join the 26th of July Movement. Several hundred appear to have enlisted under Castro's banners before the end of December, although only a small number participated in military actions.

The Communist party benefited uniquely from Castro's victory. The other established political organizations, which had been badly discredited as corrupt and incapable of resistance to the dictatorship, were rejected by the Castro movement and by the public in general. The Communists, however, as a result of their belated attachment to the revolution, escaped this fate, emerging with *de facto* legal status as the only active political party on the island. Within a week after Batista's flight into exile the Communist daily newspaper *Hoy* resumed publication, party leaders emerged from the underground, and party offices began reopening throughout Cuba. The full Communist propaganda apparatus echoed and encouraged the hysterical mass adulation of Fidel Castro which characterized the first weeks of the new regime. In the face of the almost universal affection lavished upon him, Castro could not regard the small Communist party as a serious rival for power. On the contrary, the party seemed harmless, while its open activities could be represented as proof that political liberties had been restored in Cuba.

Despite the appearance of harmony between them, the 26th of July Movement and the Communist party were not entirely compatible during the early months of the Castro administration.

Communist efforts to insinuate the party into the top leadership of the labor movement were rebuffed in March 1959, while the agrarian-reform law issued in May was criticized by Communist leaders on the grounds that it sought to move too quickly toward collectivization of agriculture. In the Soviet-approved fashion, the party called for a cautious, two-stage process of land reform patterned after the experience of the Communist states in Central Europe. Under the circumstances, the Communists, although professing approval of the regime, competed with the 26th of July Movement for the support of labor and of the peasantry.

The emergence of the Popular Socialist Party as a major prop of the revolutionary government may be attributed largely to Fidel Castro, who turned increasingly to the Communists for organizational support to offset growing disaffection within his own entourage. Many moderates and anticommunists within the 26th of July Movement were disillusioned by the steady leftward drift of the regime, with the result that the defection of prominent government figures had become commonplace before the end of 1959. Almost without exception the defectors were replaced by men more amenable to cooperation with the Communist party. In October Fidel Castro intervened personally, over the objections of labor leaders from the 26th of July Movement, to place Communists on the directing council of the Revolutionary Cuban Labor Confederation. Such actions accelerated the shift in the political orientation of the regime, strengthening the Communist party at the expense of the 26th of July Movement, and thereby increasing Castro's dependence upon Communist backing.

At the Eighth Congress of the Popular Socialist Party in August 1960, the Cuban Communists publicly proclaimed their complete solidarity with the Castro revolution. Communist leaders were exuberant over the course of events which had made the party the most powerful political organization in Cuba in less than two years. Blas Roca devoted special attention to an analysis of the six major characteristics of the revolution, which he described in the following terms:

1. the success of the rebel army proved that in a prolonged struggle guerrilla forces could be transformed into a people's revolutionary army capable of defeating a "professional army trained and supplied by Yankee imperialists";
2. the Cuban revolution destroyed the entire apparatus of the former government, and was replacing it with new institutions;
3. the revolution displaced some classes from power and installed others who initiated the "revolutionary regime of national liberation, agrarian reform, and social progress";
4. the Cuban revolution overthrew the "political domination of North American imperialism" in Cuba, thus "disproving all theories of geographic fatalism" which hold that Latin America must align with the United States because of a common location in the Western Hemisphere;
5. the Cuban revolution is taking place at a time when the world power situation and the strength of the Communist bloc has permitted Cuba to flout the will of the United States; and
6. the unity of the revolutionary forces in Cuba made the revolution and the Castro regime invincible. Significantly, Roca also noted that the Cuban revolution was not a Communist revolution, although it was "creating the conditions for its advance to the new tasks which social progress would impose upon it."

The virtually total identification of the Communist party with a noncommunist revolution and its leadership was unprecedented in Latin America and surpassed comparable statements by local Communist parties elsewhere in the world. Fidel Castro was depicted in heroic proportions as a revolutionary leader and organizer who deserved full responsibility for the success of the revolution and its program. There was no indication, however, that party leaders either looked upon Castro as a Communist or expected him to become one.

At that time Castro's value to the Cuban party and the international Communist movement lay precisely in the fact that he was not a Communist. His revolution had had an electrifying effect on liberals, leftists, and the discontented without clear political leanings from one end of Latin America to the other. By identifying themselves with such a popular, indigenous revolution, the Communists could reach a far-larger audience than at any time in the history of the movement in Latin America.

For nearly two years the Cuban revolution was presented as proof of the sincerity of Communist promises to support "revolutions of national liberation" regardless of the political leanings of the revolutionary leadership. By December 1961, when Castro declared himself a Marxist-Leninist, the Communists had gained firm control of the state and military apparatus in Cuba. The existence of Cuba as a "Socialist republic" closely tied to the Soviet camp compensated in large measure for the waning support of the revolution elsewhere in Latin America.

From the viewpoint of the international Communist movement, Cuba's chief value is as a regional propaganda and training center for Communists and leftists in the Western Hemisphere. This process had begun even before Soviet leaders decided to underwrite the Castro regime and was well developed before Castro publicly committed his government to the Communist cause. From the outset Castro's regime sought to win the support and cooperation of public figures and influential groups throughout Latin America. In the beginning this required little effort by Cuban officials. With the success of the revolution the island was deluged by thousands of well wishers and curiosity seekers from the other republics caught up in the wave of popular enthusiasm that accompanied the fall of the Batista dictatorship. Most of the visitors went to Cuba for a short time to observe, and usually to applaud the work of the new government, although many of them remained to take part in the revolutionary experiment. Citizens from every country in Latin America were incorporated into the teaching corps, the news services, and other sections of the sprawling bureaucracy maintained by the Castro administration.

As the character of the regime changed, becoming increasingly leftist, the nature of the visitors to Cuba reflected a similar shift. Before the end of 1960 the disillusioned noncommunist idealists began leaving the island and the number of incoming visitors traveling on their own initiative sharply declined. They were replaced, however, by Communists, procommunists, and useful innocents invited to Cuba at the expense of the regime. Beginning in 1960 vast amounts of international Communist financial and technical support were poured into propaganda and organizational activities in Cuba. The republic became the site of frequent Latin American youths', student, women's, and labor congresses, and a regular meeting place for Communist and other delegates en route to and from international Communist-front conferences abroad. Communist and revolutionary parties in other Latin American countries were encouraged to send members to Cuba for extensive and intensive training in administrative and organizational techniques and in military and paramilitary operations. Similar training for selected Communist party members continues to be provided in the Sino-Soviet bloc, but since the early 1960's the bulk of such trainees from Latin America has been sent to Cuba.

Shortly after coming to power the Castro administration launched a continuing program to spread the message of the revolution to the rest of Latin America. Perhaps the most effective propaganda was presented in the writings and speeches of visitors returning from Cuba, but this voluntary channel was quickly supplemented by several new instruments and by existing institutions modified to serve the purposes of the Castro regime. The first of the new agencies was the Latin American wire service *Prensa Latina,* established in the spring of 1959. It was well received initially because it seemed to fill a long-felt need in Latin America for a news service which concentrated on regional events and because its services were supplied free of charge to many small newspapers. Ostensibly the news agency was a private concern financed by Mexican and other non-Cuban businessmen and managed chiefly by Argentines. Within a year, however, it was obvious that the Havana-based *Prensa Latina* was little more than a propaganda organ for the Castro government and a relay for news and propaganda from the Communist bloc. It continued to be used by Communist, leftist, and small apolitical newspapers, but the major subscribers in most of Latin America rejected it as biased and unreliable. To offset this loss the Castro regime in 1961 inaugurated a large-scale radiobroadcasting operation designed to reach nearly all of Latin America.

In the early days of the regime pro-Cuba organizations sprang up in many Latin American countries to generate and direct popular sympathy for the Castro government. Some of these were created by noncommunists, but from the beginning they were heavily infiltrated by Communists. By the end of 1960 the pro-Cuba societies throughout Latin America were simple extensions of the Communist propaganda apparatus. The pro-Cuba activities of the front groups and the local operations of the news agency were reinforced and largely directed by Cuban diplomats in Latin America. Under Castro the Cuban diplomatic service was transformed into a propaganda and espionage arm of the regime. Cuban ambassadors became organizers and paymasters of propagandists and secret agents in much of Latin America, while tons of propaganda materials printed in the Soviet bloc and Cuba were shipped into most of the republics through the diplomatic pouch in violation of the letter and spirit of existing treaties. Activities of this nature helped to provoke all but five of the Latin American governments to break relations with Cuba during the first three years of the Castro administration, thus forcing him to rely more heavily upon the local support of Communist parties and front organizations throughout the area. These had already become *de facto* agitation and propaganda instruments at the service of the Castro government after the Soviet Union, in 1960, indicated support for Cuba as the top priority for the Latin American Communist movement.

The Castro administration has by no means confined its espousal of revolution in Latin America to propaganda activities alone. Castro and his followers came to power convinced that the Cuban revolution was the prototype of the national revolution destined to sweep over all of Latin America. The Cuban leaders, moreover, felt obligated to assist in this process, throwing the island open to like-minded revolutionaries from other countries who used it as a base for attacks on neighboring republics. During 1959 attention was focused primarily on the remaining dictatorships and governments described by Castro as "reactionary" —the Dominican Republic, Haiti, Nicaragua, Panama, and Paraguay. Between April and December of that year, invasion forces trained and armed in Cuba were sent against the first four of these countries and at least moral support was provided to rebels in Paraguay. The complete failure of these attempts caused the Castro government to alter its tactics but not its objectives. In fact, while Castro now proclaimed that the revolution was not and could not be for export, the list of target countries was expanded to include nearly all of Latin America. The existing, well-publicized training camps in Cuba were closed, but the regime continued, secretly, to instruct aspiring revolutionaries in sabotage and guerrilla warfare.

The early, massive build-up of Soviet-bloc arms in Cuba contributed both to secure the regime's position at home and to the campaign to spark revolution elsewhere in Latin America. By the end of 1960 Castro had imported a sufficient quantity of firearms to preserve his government against revolt by the Cuban people and anything less than a full-scale invasion from abroad. As Cuban forces were re-equipped with Czech and Soviet weapons, the large arsenal of United States-manufactured arms inherited from the Batista regime was released for distribution to revolutionary bands training in Cuba and other Latin American republics. In the fifth year of the Castro administration small guerrilla forces—largely supplied with arms from Cuba and led by men trained in Cuba—were active in parts of Central America, Venezuela, Colombia, Ecuador, and Peru. In other South American countries individuals trained in Cuban-guerrilla tactics were advocating the use of violence to establish governments patterned after the Cuban model. For the most part such guerrillas and would-be guerrillas were Communists and procommunists responsive to broad guidance from international Communist leaders and to direct orders from Cuba. This situation was revealed clearly in February 1963 in Venezuela, where a wave of terror and sabotage was unleashed in response to commands issued in Havana.

The success of the Cuban revolution and the subsequent course of the Castro regime have given the Sino-Soviet dispute greater significance than it would otherwise have had for the Latin American Communists. Under ordinary circumstances the Latin American parties could have been expected to endorse the

Soviet view without a murmur of dissent. Latin American Communist leaders attending the Moscow Meeting of Communist and Workers' parties late in 1960 did reaffirm their loyalty to the Soviet Union, but with some reluctance and at the cost of considerable discontent among younger members in a few parties. No Latin American Communist advocates a break with Moscow, but many of them are dissatisfied with what they interpret as an "evolutionary" approach to power proposed by the Soviet Union for the parties of the area. By and large the established leaders, conditioned to blind acceptance of Soviet directives, prefer to avoid undue risks but have been forced to accede to pressure from their impatient followers or jeopardize their control over the party. In Chile, for example, where Communist electoral prospects seem bright, party leaders discourage violence as a political method, but they have long employed a virulent anti-United States, pro-Castro propaganda line, at least in part to placate the rank and file. In Venezuela, where the old leadership insisted on pursuing the "peaceful road" despite a decline in Communist strength and the existence of a large, noncommunist *fidelista* movement, the party split over the issue. The revolutionary activities of the younger Communists led the government to outlaw all Communist factions late in 1963.

These differences over strategy and tactics are seen as ambivalence in the statements and policies of the Castro regime. Castro and other spokesmen for the Cuban government have declared publicly and repeatedly that Cuba's survival as a "Socialist republic" depends upon the continued support of the Soviet Union. Castro cannot afford to take any irreversible actions which threaten to jeopardize that support; however, by the same token the Soviet Union is obliged to tolerate an unusual degree of autonomy in Cuba or risk the loss of its only base in the Western Hemisphere. In view of his dependence upon Soviet cooperation and good will, Castro has grudgingly acknowledged the validity of the Soviet thesis of "peaceful transition to socialism," but his personal experience inclines him strongly toward the Chinese position on the use of violence. In an address to the

Congress of Women of the Americas on January 15, 1963, he expressed his attitude in these terms:

> We do not deny the possibility of peaceful transition, but we are still awaiting the first case. We do not deny it because we are not dogmatists . . . but we do say that there was no peaceful transition [in Cuba]; and we protest against an attempt to use the case of Cuba to confuse the revolutionaries of other countries where the objective conditions for the revolution exist and where they can do the same thing Cuba did. We know there are countries in which those objective conditions do not exist. . . . But they exist in the majority of the Latin American countries. That is our opinion.

The irony of Castro's position—which is not lost on other Latin American Communist leaders—is that Cuba is a prime example of "peaceful transition" to socialism. Neither Castro's acquiescence in the Communist take over of his revolution nor his own conversion to communism after he had come to power can alter the fact that the transition from noncommunist to Communist rule in Cuba was accomplished without major violence.

While the Soviet Union remains the strongest Communist power, there is little possibility that any Communist party in Latin America will give unqualified support to the Chinese Communist position. Yet, as long as Castro continues as the most successful advocate of Marxism-Leninism in Latin America, those members of other Communist parties who espouse the use of violence can expect to receive aid and comfort from the Cuban regime. In this way the Castro government in Cuba—the monument to Soviet presence in the Western Hemisphere—serves to keep alive the echoes of the Sino-Soviet dispute within the Latin American Communist movement.

TEN

Soviet-Bloc Relations with the Latin American States

SOVIET INTEREST IN LATIN AMERICA INCREASED SHARPLY AFTER THE death of Stalin in 1953 and has assumed major proportions since 1959. While expressed as friendly and disinterested concern for the welfare of the peoples of Latin America, the campaign by the Soviet Union to expand diplomatic, commercial, and cultural relations with the Latin American republics is an integral part of its effort to undermine foreign sources of support for the United States. The overriding Soviet objective in the area is to weaken or destroy Latin American cooperation with the United States—in international organizations during the cold war and as military allies in the event of global conflict. By and large this long-range goal is compatible with the immediate interests of the Latin American Communist parties, but these are invariably subordinated when they clash with the demands of Soviet foreign policy.

The Soviet Union and the other countries of the Sino-Soviet bloc are pursuing a number of mutually reinforcing tactics which complement the efforts of the local Communist parties to influence Latin American governments. Local and international Communist spokesmen and propaganda vehicles maintain a coordinated campaign to exploit Latin American sensitivities about the economic backwardness of the area, seeking to arouse unrealistic aspirations and expectations for trade and developmental assistance. They portray the United States as responsible for and indifferent to the problems of Latin America, while they represent the Communist camp as a virtually limitless market for Latin American exports and a ready source of industrial products, loans,

191

and technological aid "without political strings." Since 1960 the Soviet bloc has underwritten the Castro regime and has consistently sought to present "Socialist" Cuba as conclusive evidence that the Communist approach to rapid social and economic progress is both feasible and appropriate for Latin America. The Communist bloc has placed particular emphasis on its efforts to increase diplomatic contacts, suggesting that the establishment or renewal of diplomatic relations would greatly facilitate expansion of trade to the advantage of Latin America.

This campaign has been somewhat offset by the known proclivity of Soviet and Soviet-bloc diplomats for engaging in subversive activities and by the growing awareness in some Latin American countries that trade with the Communist nations carries with it certain disadvantages. Since 1953, nonetheless, the number of Communist-bloc diplomatic missions in Latin America has grown considerably, trade with the Communist states has become significant in Argentina, Brazil, and Uruguay, and since 1961 the Communist camp has replaced the United States as Cuba's principal trading partner.

Nationalism, in both its positive and negative aspects, has been an important influence on those Latin American leaders who have decided to establish or resume relations with Communist governments. From the viewpoint of the Latin American advocates of closer relations with the Communist bloc, a decisive consideration is the possibility—usually presented as a certainty —that the Communist countries will prove to be a vast market for surplus export commodities and a major source of economic-development funds. In short, the bloc is viewed as a promising additional source of aid and trade. At the same time, the establishment of relations with Communist powers is a sovereign act which the Latin American republics can take to demonstrate their "independence" from the United States. Clearly, both the attraction of anticipated economic benefits and the desire to make a dramatic gesture of national sovereignty were involved in the decision to expand ties with the Communist bloc by Castro in 1960 and by Presidents Quadros and Goulart of Brazil in 1961. Actions of this nature—or merely the promise of such actions—

are usually certain to elicit popular support for the administration and may be calculated to improve the country's bargaining position with the United States. Even such avowed anticommunists as Trujillo of the Dominican Republic and Duvalier of Haiti threatened in the early 1960's to turn to the Communist camp in efforts to extract favorable treatment from this country. Other Latin American leaders have generally been more subtle in the use of this gambit, but all of them are keenly aware that the emergence of the Communist states as a major world-power complex has given them a potential alternative to dependence upon the United States.

The pattern of Soviet diplomatic relations with Latin America has fluctuated in much the same manner as the fortunes of the local Communist parties. Prior to the second world war only three Latin American nations granted *de jure* recognition to the Soviet Union. The first of these was Mexico, which established relations in August 1924, in the waning months of the Obrégon administration. For more than five years there was a Soviet legation in Mexico City and a comparable Mexican mission in Moscow. Three weeks after the inauguration of President Ortiz Rubio in January 1930, however, Mexico suddenly severed relations with the Soviet Union, following a rash of anti-Mexican demonstrations by Communists in Berlin, Buenos Aires, Rio de Janeiro, Washington, and other capitals in Europe and the Americas. In South America the first Soviet diplomatic post was a legation set up in Montevideo shortly after the establishment of formal relations with Uruguay in August 1926. In the absence of significant trade or political ties between the two countries, Uruguay did not open a mission in the Soviet capital. The chief function of the Soviet legation was apparently to complement the efforts of Iumtorg and the South American Bureau of the Comintern as a link between the Soviet Union and the Communist parties of Uruguay, Paraguay, Argentina, Chile, Peru, and Brazil. Uruguayan-Soviet relations were maintained until December 1935, when they were broken by Uruguay on the grounds of a Communist threat to the country. The primary cause for the rupture appears to have been strong pressure from Brazil for expulsion of the Soviet mission, which had contributed to the Communist-led revolt against the Vargas regime in November of that year. Earlier, in June 1935, Colombia had established relations with the Soviet Union, and until 1942 Bogotá was host to the only Soviet diplomatic post in all of Latin America.

The participation of the Soviet Union and the Latin American republics as Allies in World War II produced a favorable climate for the expansion of diplomatic contacts. Between 1942 and 1945 thirteen Latin American countries established relations or extended formal recognition to the Soviet government. Several of them were encouraged by the United States to take such action as a gesture of wartime solidarity. Cuba began the new trend, establishing relations at the embassy level in October 1942. One month later Mexico resumed relations, also at the embassy level. The importance attached by the Soviet Union to the Mexican post was revealed in the assignment, in June 1943, of a top diplomat and former ambassador to the United States, Constantine Oumansky, as ambassador to Mexico. For two decades the Embassy in Mexico City was to be the major center of Soviet activities in Latin America. At the other end of the hemisphere, the Soviet legation in Montevideo was reopened in January 1943, when the Uruguayan government renewed relations after a lapse of more than six years. Uruguay was one of two Latin American republics to establish diplomatic ties with the Soviet Union before entering the second world war. The other was Chile, which agreed in December 1944 to exchange ambassadors with the Soviet regime. Within the next four months, following the Inter-American Conference on Problems of War and Peace which met at Chapultepec early in 1945, Venezuela and Brazil recognized the Soviet Union and arranged to exchange ambassadors. The Venezuelan action was taken in March and that of Brazil in April of 1945. Previously the governments of Costa Rica and Nicaragua, in May and December 1944 respectively, had recognized the Soviet Union but made no provisions for resident diplomatic missions. The same procedure was followed by the Dominican Republic in March, by Bolivia, Guatemala, and El Salvador in April, and by Ecuador in June 1945.

The high point in Soviet diplomatic relations with Latin America was reached in 1946, following the decision in June of that year by the Perón regime in Argentina to exchange ambassadors with the Soviet government. At that time, before the wartime spirit of good feeling between East and West had begun to wane, the Soviet Union was formally recognized by fifteen of the twenty Latin American republics. In eight of these there were resident Soviet missions—the legation in Uruguay and seven Embassies—which served the dual purpose of conducting legitimate state-to-state relations while providing secure channels of communication and support between Moscow and the Communist parties of the area.

The opening of the cold war in 1947 reversed the upward trend in the number of Soviet missions in Latin America. During the next eight years—which witnessed the final phase of Stalin's intransigent rule over the Communist empire and the resurgence of dictatorships in much of Latin America—all but three of the fifteen republics that had recognized the Soviet government broke relations or denied that relations existed with the Soviet Union. In each case a specific grievance was cited as justification for the action taken. In most instances, however, the decision to cut formal ties with the Communist power reflected the broad anticommunist policies being adopted by the Latin American governments, at least in part to win favor with the United States.

In October 1947 both Brazil and Chile broke relations with the Soviet Union, closing their Embassies in Moscow and expelling Soviet diplomats from their national territory. During the same year the government of Ecuador announced flatly that it did not maintain relations with the Soviet regime. Subsequent administrations in Quito, moreover, have consistently upheld this attitude, although the Soviet Union continues to include Ecuador in its published diplomatic list. Colombia abruptly severed its ties in May 1948, one day after the closing session of the Ninth Inter-American Conference, which had been interrupted by a violent riot involving the Communists in Bogotá. The following month the Costa Rican government stated that it did not desire to continue relations with the Soviet Union. Although the Soviet ambassador to Mexico had been accredited as envoy to Costa Rica, there was no resident Soviet mission in San José, nor had Costa Rican diplomats been sent to Moscow. In a comparable situation, the Dominican Republic severed formal ties simply by stating that relations with the Soviet Union did not exist. Cuba provoked a break in relations in April 1952, less than one month after Batista seized power, and Venezuela, under Dictator-President Pérez Jiménez, did the same in June of that year. In El Salvador the Osorio regime, which came to power in 1952, issued a formal denial of relations with the Soviet government and was dropped from the Soviet diplomatic list. Guatemala broke relations in July 1954, shortly after the overthrow of the Communist-dominated Arbenz administration. (The Soviet Union was believed to have been responsible for a shipment of Czech arms to the Arbenz regime earlier in the year.) At the end of the following year the Bolivian Foreign Ministry indicated that the republic did not maintain relations with the Soviet Union. Bolivia, too, however, has continued to appear regularly in the Soviet diplomatic list as a country with which formal relations exist. In the case of Nicaragua the relations established in 1944 have never been implemented.

Of the governments that have broken with the Soviet Union since 1947, only Cuba and Brazil have re-established relations, in May 1960 and November 1961, respectively. Elsewhere there has been a great deal of pressure on several governments, particularly those of Venezuela, Bolivia, and Chile, for the renewal of ties with Moscow. The Bolivian legislature in 1958 went so far as to appropriate funds for the creation of an Embassy in the Soviet capital, but for several years the administration has pointedly failed to act on this suggestion. In general, governments under such pressure have indicated that the establishment of formal diplomatic contacts with the Soviet Union is not currently in the national interest. Five Latin American republics— Haiti, Honduras, Panama, Paraguay, and Peru—have never recognized the Soviet Union.

Since the mid-1950's, with the change in Soviet leadership, policies, and power position, and with the return to more representative governments in much of Latin America, there has been a sharp upturn in the establishment of relations with Communist regimes. The emphasis, however, has been on the formation of diplomatic ties with the countries of the Soviet bloc rather than with the Soviet Union itself. In the immediate postwar period several of the Latin American republics initiated diplomatic contacts with the newly Communist countries of Eastern Europe or permitted relations dating from the prewar era to continue with the new regimes. By 1956 there was a total of sixteen Communist resident diplomatic posts in seven countries, including the Soviet Embassies in Mexico and Argentina and the legation in Uruguay. All the satellite diplomatic missions were legations. Czechoslovakia was represented in Argentina, Bolivia, Brazil, Ecuador, Mexico, Peru, and Uruguay. Polish legations were established in Argentina, Brazil, and Mexico. In addition, the Polish Minister to Mexico was accredited to Colombia, Costa Rica, Ecuador, Haiti, Honduras, Nicaragua, and Panama, but no resident staffs were located in these countries. Bulgaria, Hungary, and Rumania maintained resident missions in Buenos Aires, while the Hungarian Minister was also accredited to Uruguay and Bolivia. Nondiplomatic posts included a Czech Consulate-General in Bogotá and three Polish Consulates in Brazil.

Through the rest of the decade of the 1950's the distribution of Soviet-bloc missions in Latin America was modified slightly, but the number remained fairly constant from year to year. The closing of Czech legations in Peru and Ecuador in 1957 was offset by the opening that year of a Rumanian legation in Uruguay and the addition, in 1958, of a Czech Consulate in Monterrey, Mexico. A major breakthrough occurred, however, in the early 1960's, when the number of separate diplomatic and consular posts more than doubled, to a total of thirty-nine in nine countries. The major change took place in Cuba, which established relations in 1960 with eleven Sino-Soviet–bloc countries—all except East Germany. By the end of the year ten of these—the Soviet Union, Albania, Bulgaria, Czechoslovakia, Hungary, Poland, Rumania, Communist China, North Korea, and North

Vietnam—had opened Embassies in Havana. A Mongolian Embassy was established in Havana in 1962. As a practical matter the East German trade mission in Havana, technically a nondiplomatic post, served as an Embassy in all but name. Thus, under Castro, Cuba became the only Latin American republic to recognize Communist China and one of the few nations in the world to maintain relations with every Communist regime.

The Soviet bloc has more diplomatic and consular posts in Brazil than in any other Latin American country except Cuba. In 1961 Brazil renewed relations with the Soviet Union, resumed formal contacts with Hungary and Rumania for the first time since World War II, and established its first diplomatic ties with Albania and Bulgaria. The Soviet Embassy and the four new satellite legations opened during 1961 and the early months of 1962, and in the same period, previously established Czech and Polish legations were raised to embassy status as a reflection of the Brazilian policy of upgrading the level of its diplomatic representation. The Brazilian government also approved the elevation of the Polish Consulates in São Paulo and Curitiba to Consulates-General and the opening of a new Polish Consulate in Pôrto Alegre. Prior to the formal resumption of relations with the Soviet Union in November 1961, the Brazilian government finally canceled the credentials of the Latvian and Lithuanian Ministers and the Estonian Consul, all of whom had been representing governments-in-exile since the second world war.

Elsewhere, changes in diplomatic relations involved four Latin American republics and three Soviet-bloc regimes. Mexico concluded agreements with Czechoslovakia and Poland, raising their respective legations to embassy rank. In 1960, new Polish and Bulgarian legations were opened in Uruguay and, for the first time since before World War II, Venezuela resumed relations with Poland, at the embassy level. The Czech legation in Quito reopened in 1960 but was closed again in 1962, when Ecuador broke relations with Czechoslovakia.

The outsized staffs assigned to Soviet-bloc missions and the penchant of Communist diplomats for meddling in domestic politics have frequently led to public protests and friction in

Latin American relations with the bloc. The interference of Czech diplomats in internal political and labor matters in Peru and Ecuador in 1957 provoked a rupture in relations with the Peruvian government and the expulsion of the staff of the legation from Quito. Two years later a rash of intolerable activity by Soviet and satellite diplomats in Mexico and Argentina strained relations but did not lead to an open break. Mexico requested the recall of two officials of the Soviet Embassy for involvement in a national railroad strike, while Argentina declared a total of five bloc diplomats *persona non grata* for similar offenses and expelled the Bulgarian Minister for operating a clandestine radio transmitter in the legation. In 1962 Ecuador severed formal ties with Czechoslovakia and Cuba on grounds that diplomats from those nations were encouraging subversion among Ecuadoran leftists. During these years there was mounting popular pressure on the governments of Mexico, Argentina, and Uruguay to force a substantial reduction in the size of the Soviet missions, to make them comparable with the small staffs these countries maintain in Moscow. It is widely assumed that the scores of diplomats and attachés assigned to posts in Latin America are engaged primarily in Communist propaganda and espionage activities rather than in the normal conduct of relations between nations. The Frondizi administration in Argentina placed travel restrictions on Soviet and Rumanian personnel and called on all of the Soviet-bloc governments to reduce drastically the number of individuals sent to their missions in Buenos Aires. The Brazilian government in 1961 sought to forestall opposition to the resumption of relations with the Soviet Union by imposing a limit on the number of Soviet diplomats that might be assigned to the country and by confining them to a radius of 35 kilometers from the Embassy.

The considerable rise in the level of bloc diplomatic relations with Latin America is a measure of the success of the Soviet-trade offensive in the area since the death of Stalin. It also reflects the enhanced appreciation by the Latin American governments of the economic and military power of the Soviet Union since the launching of the first sputnik in 1957. Further, the ability of the Soviet bloc to absorb most Cuban exports and to supply the bulk of essential imports to the Castro regime has strengthened the impression of many Latin Americans that the Communist world is both able and willing to become a major trading partner.

The Communist camp still accounts for only a small percentage of Latin America's total trade, although both the volume and share of trade with the Soviet bloc rose sharply with the reorientation of the Cuban economy in 1961. Latin American trade with the Communist countries surpassed $200 million for the first time in 1954, when the area's commerce with the world approximated $15 billion. Eight years later these figures were on the order of $1 billion and $20 billion, respectively. Cuba is by far the leading Latin American republic in trade with the bloc. Brazil ranks second, while Argentina and Uruguay account for nearly all the remainder. These four countries confine their trade with the bloc largely to Czechoslovakia, Poland, and the Soviet Union, although each of the four has commercial agreements with other Communist countries as well. Since 1960 Cuba has entered into at least one commercial agreement with every Communist regime.

Argentina was the first country in Latin America to develop a significant volume of trade with the Soviet bloc. Such trade reached 9 per cent of Argentine commerce with the world in the last year of the Perón regime, but since 1955 it has dropped to an average of about 5 per cent annually. Argentina offers modest quantities of its traditional exports—meat, wheat, linseed oil, wool, hides, and quebracho extract—which are usually in oversupply, in exchange for semiprocessed metals, industrial and business machines, lumber, fuels, and chemicals. The imports come chiefly from Czechoslovakia and Poland, although from time to time Hungarian railroad equipment and Soviet petroleum have figured as major items from the bloc. Successive administrations in Argentina have sought to counter the tendency to run a credit balance with the Soviet bloc by encouraging imports and by shifting from bilateral to multilateral trade arrangements with the Communist states.

Prior to the Cuban revolution Uruguay committed a higher percentage of its trade to the Soviet bloc than did any other Latin American nation. The level of direct trade with Communist countries, which had been at about 5 per cent, rose to over 16 per cent in 1958 and 1959, when the Soviet Union purchased large quantities of Uruguayan wool. Bloc purchases made indirectly through Western Europe lifted the total to well over one-fourth of all Uruguayan exports during these years. This was a period of declining world markets for Uruguayan exports in which the country was faced simultaneously with a surplus of wool and a serious shortage of foreign exchange. Under the circumstances Uruguay shifted most of its petroleum imports from Western sources, which required hard currencies, to the Soviet Union under what was essentially a barter deal. By 1959, however, the Uruguayan government was becoming concerned over the trend and resisted Soviet overtures for an even greater share of the nation's trade. In an effort to force Uruguay to agree to the exchange of additional petroleum for wool, the Soviet Union in 1960 refused to buy any Uruguayan wool. At the same time all other Communist regimes except Communist China reduced their purchases from Uruguay. This action cut the level of bloc trade to about 10 per cent of Uruguay's foreign commerce and made Communist China the principal bloc trading partner during that year. Uruguay was able to resist Communist pressure in this instance because of a rise in the world wool market and a modification of United States tariff regulations that had barred much Uruguayan wool from this country. Since 1960 the level of Uruguay's trade with the Soviet bloc has continued to decline.

Brazil's trade with the Soviet bloc has fluctuated over the years since 1953 but has been in a sharply rising trend since 1959, when it first reached the $100 million level. By 1962 it had doubled the previous high. This was a reflection of the Brazilian policy of increasing trade with all areas, which had become a major political issue in the presidential campaign of 1960. Under Presidents Quadros and Goulart in 1961, Brazil arranged for new commercial agreements with the Soviet Union, Communist

China, and all the Communist countries of Europe. Brazil's commerce with the Communist camp is limited largely, however, to Czechoslovakia, Poland, and the Soviet Union. It involves the exchange of coffee, cacao, fibers, iron ore, hides, and vegetable oils for petroleum and wheat from the Soviet Union, ships, rails, and railroad equipment from Poland, and a range of industrial machinery and other manufactured articles from the three countries. Soviet and Polish technicians have also been accepted by Brazil to assist in industrial-development projects.

Before 1959 Cuba's economic relations with the Soviet bloc were limited and sporadic, consisting chiefly of occasional large exports of sugar to the Soviet Union in exchange for hard currencies. Imports of consumer goods from Czechoslovakia were insignificant in the total Cuban-trade pattern. Since the rise of Castro, however, this pattern has been almost entirely reversed. Cuba sold half a million tons of sugar to the Soviet Union in 1959 and over two million tons in 1960. Since 1960 the Soviet bloc and Communist China have taken the bulk of all Cuban exports and have become the major suppliers of imports which previously came from the United States, Western Europe, and Venezuela. By 1961 the Communist states accounted for at least 85 per cent of Cuba's total trade. In addition to vast quantities of military equipment, the bloc has provided Cuba with long-term credits, loans, and technical assistance on a large scale. Cuba continues to trade with some countries of the free world in order to obtain those items that are not available from Communist sources. In the process Cuban commerce with Latin America has shown a large percentage increase, although by volume it is still small. Petroleum imports from Venezuela have ceased altogether.

Each of the other sixteen republics of Latin America has carried on some trade with the Communist world since 1953, but the total is insignificant. Paraguay and Haiti are the only ones whose commerce with the Soviet bloc has ever amounted to more than 1 per cent of their foreign trade. In each instance this peak was reached in the mid-1950's, and has since declined. Mexico has a trade-and-payments agreement with Czechoslovakia, and Colombia has commercial agreements with several Soviet-bloc regimes. Elsewhere the exchange of Latin American coffee, minerals, and fibers for consumer goods and industrial equipment from the bloc is conducted on an *ad hoc* basis.

The arguments for and against expanded trade with the Communist camp are still being debated vociferously throughout much of Latin America. Bloc trade is presented by its Communist and noncommunist advocates as a panacea for Latin America's economic ills. Its proponents claim that expansion of commerce with the Soviet bloc will relieve chronic pressure on balance of payments by providing new markets for otherwise unsalable export surpluses and an important nondollar source of certain imports essential for industrial development. This appeal continues to be highly attractive to hard-pressed government officials and to politicians seeking a popular following. It is being weakened somewhat, however, by increased awareness of the practical problems that have arisen in countries which conduct a significant volume of trade with the Communist world. One of the principal drawbacks stems from the fact that under the standard twelve-month commercial agreements, exports and imports are expected to balance each year. Thus, the Latin American countries can dispose of their surplus commodities in the Communist market only to the extent that they increase their imports of bloc merchandise. In these circumstances there is a trend toward longer-term agreements to provide greater flexibility in import-export balances. A closely related difficulty is caused by the Communist practice of conducting all commerce through state agencies. These can deal easily only with comparable organizations—government ministries and agencies such as those created in Cuba under Castro. Consequently, it is not surprising that the Latin American governments themselves are the principal importers of bloc goods, while private firms generally prefer to continue to do business with suppliers in the West. The quality and delivery terms of Soviet-bloc articles, moreover, are not always competitive with similar items from free-world sources. This situation further contributes to the resistance of the private sector against any substantial increase in imports of consumer goods from Communist countries. Where Latin America's foreign trade is handled largely by private enterprise, such resistance would seem to place definite limits on the potential level of trade with the Soviet bloc.

In conjunction with the campaign to increase commercial and diplomatic relations with Latin America the Communist states have pursued an active campaign for closer cultural contacts between the two areas. By and large the cultural offensive—which can be presented convincingly as "nonpolitical"—has encountered less opposition than the trade drive and the efforts to expand diplomatic ties. Even fervent anticommunists can usually detect little immediate threat to Latin American institutions in visits by outstanding Communist artists, musicians, or athletes; nevertheless, they may protest against agreements calling for distribution of Soviet literature or for frequent exhibits of Communist-bloc films as undesirable propaganda. Many well-educated Latin Americans who deplore the Communist political and economic systems frankly admire Soviet advances in the arts and sciences and the high prestige enjoyed by artists and men of letters in Soviet society. With respect to the latter they tend to regard Soviet custom as less alien than that of the United States —a tendency which foreign and local Communists exploit to advantage.

The cultural campaign is an integral part of the over-all Communist propaganda effort, designed to present a favorable view of the Soviet camp to all sectors of Latin American society. Thus, it makes use of the full range of propaganda vehicles available to the local and international Communist movement in the area. Soviet-bloc cultural relations with Latin America are fostered by an intensive exchange of persons, information, and techniques between government officials, scholars, artists, and members of the professions. An effective device is scholarships offered to Latin American students desiring to study scientific and technical subjects in Communist universities and industrial schools. Such scholarships are customarily for a year of instruction in the language of the host country and for five years of professional training. An impressive number of world-renowned

Soviet violinists, pianists, and ballet troupes have conducted highly successful tours of Latin America. Information about Communist culture and scientific achievements has also been presented to the general public in much of Latin America through traveling expositions, which are usually accompanied by internationally known Soviet dignitaries such as Deputy Premier Mikoyan and a succession of Soviet cosmonauts. In terms of sheer numbers, even larger crowds are attracted by the recurring festivals of Soviet and Soviet-bloc films, which are exhibited in many areas not visited by Communist personalities, and by touring basketball and soccer teams from the Communist countries of Europe.

Where formal diplomatic relations exist the Communist regimes promote cultural agreements between governments to facilitate the various categories of official and unofficial exchanges. In such instances the exchanges are usually processed through resident Soviet-bloc missions in the Latin American capitals. In the absence of diplomatic contacts, the burden of encouraging the cultural offensive is borne chiefly by local Communist-front binational centers and societies, which handle travel arrangements and disseminate large quantities of printed propaganda about artistic and professional life in the Communist world. In both situations the local Communist party lends as much assistance as possible through its press and its other front organizations. In addition, since 1960 the Castro regime in Cuba has served as an important agent in the Communist cultural drive, supplementing local and international propaganda activities and facilitating travel for citizens of countries where contacts with the Soviet bloc are discouraged by the government. A substantial volume of propaganda materials from Communist regimes is disseminated through the dwindling number of Cuban diplomatic posts and *Prensa Latina* agencies in Latin America and by travelers returning from Communist-front meetings in Cuba or in other Communist states. Citizens of all Latin American countries may reach Havana easily by way of Mexico, and continue to Eastern Europe on either the Cuban or Czech airlines. No permanent record of such travel is entered in their passports.

IV.

Problems and Prospects

The Communist Potential

THE HISTORY OF COMMUNIST ACTIVITIES OVER NEARLY HALF A century reveals the inherent strengths and weaknesses of the movement and provides a basis for projections of the future course of communism in Latin America. At the same time the frequent and dramatic reversals of Communist fortunes in the past suggest that predictions as to the future of the Communist movement are hazardous at best and must be subject to continuous review. Generalizations based on the experience of any individual Communist party are of limited applicability to Latin America as a whole, while conclusions about the over-all Communist movement are seldom equally valid for each of the twenty republics. The following appraisal of the Communist potential in Latin America should be considered with these limitations in mind.

One of the few conclusions that appears to have near-universal validity in Latin America is that Communist successes depend far more upon outside factors than upon the immediate condition of the party itself. The Communists have long recognized this fact in their insistence that they must at all times be prepared to assume direct or indirect national leadership when circumstances permit. Thus, despite the apparent hopelessness of their cause, the Latin American parties have persisted in their quest for political power, for it has been shown repeatedly that a minute, repressed Communist organization can spring into effective political action when conditions suddenly become favorable. In the early 1960's this situation was pointedly illustrated by the case of Cuba, where a fortuitous coincidence of national and international developments had enabled the party in less than five years to secure a grasp on a government that could be broken only by force of arms. In most of the other republics the Communists continued to represent only a tiny segment of the body politic. It is entirely unlikely that any other Latin American Communist organization will encounter precisely the same opportunities that were presented to the Cuban party, but for the foreseeable future most of the Latin American parties may be expected to look to the Cuban experience for inspiration and guidance and to work persistently toward the day when conditions may allow them to emulate the Cuban example.

The Latin American Communists have no control over the international developments that may be decisive in creating or destroying situations in which they might come to power. In most of the countries, moreover, they can exert little direct influence on the course of national politics. An unanticipated change on the world scene—such as a spectacular power breakthrough by the United States, or the total disruption of the Sino-Soviet bloc—could make it virtually impossible for Communist fortunes to improve significantly in Latin America regardless of actions taken by the local parties. But while the cold war endures and the power balance between East and West remains relatively stable, the Latin American Communists should continue to enjoy the same favorable international climate which permitted their comrades to gain control of Cuba. Likewise, within the Western Hemisphere, relationships between nations appear conducive to continued improvement in Communist prospects.

There is little likelihood of joint action by the members of the Organization of American States to unseat Communist or Communist-oriented regimes in Latin America. Such action is politically unfeasible as long as the governments of Brazil and Mexico—which rule over half the population of the area—continue to hold that Castro's Cuba poses no threat to themselves or to the hemispheric body and that its government represents the will of the Cuban people. Barring either a new and unmistakable Soviet military threat through Cuba or the introduction of Soviet military presence elsewhere in the hemisphere, the two leading Latin American nations may be expected to persist in these views and to insist upon unqualified observance of the policies of nonintervention and self-determination of Latin American peoples. And the restraints on the unilateral use of force by the United States to depose Communist regimes seem likely to persist indefinitely.

In the majority of the Latin American republics the tendency for population growth to outstrip increases in available resources at the same time that the underprivileged masses are insisting upon an immediate and striking improvement in their way of life promises to continue for at least a generation. The population of Latin America is expected to surpass half a billion before the end of the century. In this situation—which cannot be resolved by traditional or "reasonable" means—advocates of extremist political solutions to social and economic problems may be expected to displace moderates in national political office. It is by no means inevitable that the transition will everywhere come about by revolution. In some of the smaller countries the forces of change may be contained for an indefinite period by repressive methods, whereas elsewhere governments committed to social reforms and rapid economic development may be able to avert violent social and political upheaval. But whether by revolution or evolution, it appears certain that the political complexion of the ruling groups in most of Latin America will become increasingly leftist. In these circumstances, the distinctions—already blurred—between the programs and immediate objectives of governments and noncommunist political parties, on the one hand, and those proposed by the Communist parties, on the other, will become even more difficult to detect.

It is, therefore, not surprising that the Communists in Latin America are highly optimistic about their future prospects. They are confident not only that the trends evident since the mid-1950's will continue, but also that the rate of change will be accelerated as popular campaigns for social and political reforms gain momentum. The local parties are confident, moreover, that Cuba and the Soviet bloc will continue to provide them indispensable moral and material assistance commensurate with their needs and opportunities. In Communist calculations time is clearly on their side, and for the first time in several of the republics the party leadership has become convinced that it may actually be possible to seize power or to gain an influential voice in the government within the near future. They assert—in Marxist-Leninist terms—that the "objective conditions" for a Communist-oriented revolution already exist in much of the area and that their chief task now is to create or to hasten the emergence of the so-called "subjective conditions," i.e., a revolutionary spirit and cohesion among leftist forces, without which a Communist bid for power would be doomed to failure.

In their analysis of the outside factors conducive to drastic political change the Latin American Communists are in nearly unanimous agreement. They are divided among themselves, however, on the question of the tactics that will best accomplish their aims. Fundamentally, the difference centers on conflicting interpretations of what constitutes "subjective conditions for revolution" and the most effective methods of generating such conditions. Some Communist spokesmen advocate guerrilla warfare as the quickest and most practical method, while others, including the bulk of the top leadership in many parties, argue that in view of the strong leftist trend in Latin American politics they can come to power with less risk by pursuing a "parliamentary" course. This division of opinion reflects to a considerable degree the ideological rift between the Soviet Union and Communist China, but it is more than a regional manifestation of Sino-Soviet divergence. In a real sense it also reflects the impatience of youthful party members with the caution—in some cases, almost inertia—of older Communist leaders. And it reveals the range of political conditions that exist in the various Latin American countries. Where the Communist party remains out of power and on the fringes of national politics, these differences will almost certainly persist and the Communists will probably continue to dissipate part of their energies in fruitless debates. But it would be deceptive to assume that any Communist party will permit such bickering to blind it to opportunities to improve its position by whatever means appear most appropriate at a given moment. The parties may well split or may give the appearance of splitting in order to pursue both violent and non-violent policies simultaneously, only to coalesce again when one or the other has proved effective. In short, it may be anticipated that political opportunism and tactical flexibility will continue to be characteristic of the Latin American Communist parties.

This Machiavellian approach to politics is only one of the proven assets that have permitted the Communist parties to survive under adverse conditions in the past and that they will doubtless seek to employ to maximum advantage in the generally favorable political environment in the foreseeable future. The Communist party will probably continue to be the most tightly organized and rigidly disciplined political organization in the majority of the Latin American republics. While the range of ideologically based parties may be expected to increase in both numbers and effectiveness, it is unlikely that other Latin American parties will soon be able or be willing to extract from their members the total commitment that the Communist party demands of its adherents. That every Communist must be an active propagandist and that the party can and does maintain a broad façade of front organizations to disseminate its line in manifold guises will almost certainly permit the Communists to project an exaggerated impression of their importance. Thus, the party wherever it enjoys freedom of operation should be able, as in the past, to exert influence out of all proportion to its limited numbers.

The forecast of the continued existence and effectiveness of the Communist propaganda apparatus presumes that the appeal of communism will remain strong among opinion leaders and among much of the general public and that the tendency to accept Communists at face value will persist throughout Latin America. In this area the Communists count heavily, and realistically, on the continued support or tolerance of the intellectual community, which lends prestige to any political doctrine of which it approves. And a substantial portion of Latin American intellectuals find communism a respectable political philosophy.

The apparent universality of Communist doctrine holds, and will probably continue to hold, a fascinating attraction for those educated in the humanistic tradition of Latin American universities. In this period of profound change, when traditional values and systems are being questioned, many individuals from the Latin American intelligentsia are finding that communism provides a rational explanation for the social ferment and confusion that surrounds them. Thus, even though so very many of them have not and probably will not become Communists in the literal sense, they, as internationalists and humanitarians, encounter almost no difficulty in accepting Marxist-Leninist interpretations of history and predictions about the destiny of man. They view Latin America as part of one great world that is moving rapidly toward socialism. They interpret the collapse of old colonial empires and the advances of communism elsewhere as verification of Marxist predictions. They tend to accept uncritically Communist claims that in the continuing clash between Marxists and "reactionaries" the oppression of imperialism and the vestiges of feudalism are gradually being eliminated, and they are persuaded to hope that when these evils are finally destroyed at home and abroad the millennium will be realized. There is little reason to anticipate any dramatic change in the outlook of this group.

The Communist appeal is by no means confined to the tiny minority of university graduates in Latin American society. To a broad segment of the Latin American public, many Communist views and proposals for social, economic, and political change seem neither unreasonable nor radical. The people of Latin America may be expected to continue to approve of those Communist views which they believe to coincide with their own, and to be increasingly reluctant to object to the source of proposals since they do not object to the proposals themselves. In fact, as noted above, the programs and ultimate objectives of some noncommunist parties are already virtually indistinguishable from the avowed programs and immediate objectives of the Latin American Communists. Indeed, although the overriding concern of most Latin Americans for rapid and spectacular economic growth was not caused by Communist propaganda, the Communists have been able, nevertheless, to identify themselves with this almost universal sentiment. Moreover, the Communists have no monopoly on Marxism or on the tendency to turn to the Soviet bloc to reduce Latin American dependence on the United States. Some of the noncommunist leftist parties even equal the Communists in their opposition to capitalism and to "capitalistic imperialism." The ultranationalism of many Latin Americans and the tendency to regard the United States as an "imperialist" enemy of the Latin American people exist independently of the Communists, although their propaganda hammers incessantly on both themes. Communist denunciations of present governments for their failure to satisfy the insistent demands of an exploding populace for higher living standards are no more bitter nor vehement than attacks by noncommunist opposition parties. Far more Latin Americans than can be found in the Communist movement have lost or are losing faith in the ability of the democratic process—as it is understood in Latin America—to meet the staggering socioeconomic needs of the area. Many in addition to the Communists protest that Latin America has neither social justice, true political freedom, full national sovereignty, nor an adequate rate of economic progress. It seems clear that even without the Communists, much of the revolutionary program they advocate will be pursued in Latin America. By the same token, a large portion of the politically active population finds it only logical and proper that the Communists should participate in the common effort to achieve these objectives.

The identification of the Communist parties with the Soviet Union has in the past been at times a liability, at times an asset. On the whole, it appears that such identification should be an advantage to the Latin American Communist parties as long as the East-West power balance persists and the Soviet Union continues to register scientific and technological gains comparable to those of the Western democracies. It is clear that informed Latin Americans are deeply impressed by the increasing politico-military power and scientific prowess of the Soviet Union, and as unwavering advocates of the Marxist-Leninist solution to Latin America's problems, the Communists expect to gain enhanced prestige and authority from among the growing body of Latin American admirers of Soviet "progress." Therefore, while the Communists will undoubtedly continue to present themselves as ardent nationalists, they will probably not seek to deny or to disguise their ties with the center of world communism. Traditionally, they have followed Soviet advice— whether it was sound or not—and doubtless will continue to follow it. For the foreseeable future Communist parties that reject Soviet tutelage will be the rare exceptions in Latin America. Moreover, it is likely that Soviet foreign-policy objectives in the near future will continue to encourage local Communist bids for power, but it is equally apparent that the Latin American Communists will desist from such efforts if these should come to clash with the interests of the Soviet state.

One of the few certainties with respect to the Latin American Communist movement is that within a few years there will be widespread change in the top leadership of the parties in most of the republics. By and large the current leaders are "old" Communists, both in experience and in years, and many of them will inevitably disappear in the next decade or less. For the most part, these men have not proved to be inspiring leaders and, without exception, they have failed to draw the masses into the party. In most instances they have served as party bureaucrats, content to administer the local Communist organization according to directives set forth in Moscow. In all likelihood, where the party remains out of power and largely excluded from the political process, the outgoing figures will be replaced by younger bureaucrats who share many of the same characteristics that have marked the party leadership for a quarter century or more. Thus, it is probable that many of the top Latin American Communists will continue to lack the charisma likely to be required of heads of state in the area in coming years. Where this situation exists it may constitute a continuing liability for the party. Noncommunists, however, cannot afford to be complacent about the absence of a charismatic figure at the helm of the local Communist movement, for this liability can suddenly disappear wherever a political contest degenerates into revolution or civil war. The experiences of the party in Guatemala and Cuba suggest that the Communists will seek to cooperate closely with, and if possible to convert, any dynamic revolutionary leader willing to accept their assistance. While the rise of another latter-day Communist of Castro's stature is improbable in Latin America, it has been clearly demonstrated that the Communists can succeed by throwing their full support behind a magnetic personality who becomes dependent upon them.

If past performance is a reliable guide, the Communists in Latin America may confidently be expected to display occasional ineptness, to alienate potentially valuable allies, and perhaps to suffer adverse repercussions from exposure of Communist ruthlessness abroad. But tactical blunders at home and fleeting revelations of the nature of Soviet imperialism in other areas of the world have never done lasting injury to the Communist appeal in Latin America. Wherever their position is improving or their prospects seem bright the Communists have always been able to attract a following. They appeal successfully to those who disbelieve or ignore charges of Communist duplicity and subservience to Moscow. They attract the opportunists ready to overlook such "idiosyncracies" in order to gain short-term material rewards, and they draw the idealists who regard such characteristics as a necessary price to be paid for the eventual attainment of a "better world." Their ability to appeal to all of these groups has always been greatest when they could present the party as a legitimate, respectable, and influential participant in national politics.

The Latin American Communists—and their adversaries— are keenly aware that global, hemispheric, and national trends promise a favorable climate for Communist operations in the foreseeable future. They are also aware that in this situation the prospects for the individual parties to gain power or a share of power will depend largely on their own effectiveness in exploiting weaknesses in the sociopolitical structure of the respective republics. The Communists are confident of their ability to attract such an imposing following and to enlist such influential allies that the governments will be reluctant or unable to take effective measures against them. They are counting on their propaganda apparatus to encourage a defeatist mentality among government and noncommunist party leaders while exacerbating popular aspirations and disillusionment to the boiling point. In the Communist view it is inevitable that sooner or later they will either be accepted by desperate governments seeking to stave off revolution or be swept into power by revolution.

Although the Communists considerably exaggerate their capabilities, there are some impressive grounds for Communist optimism. Perhaps the greatest asset the party enjoys is widespread apathy and incomprehension of the danger it poses to the traditional values of Latin American culture. For the whole of their adult lives, the men in responsible positions in Latin America have been accustomed to look upon the local Communist party as a harmless body of eccentrics out of the main stream of national politics. Because in the past every Communist advance has been followed by a setback, they tend to assume that this pattern will repeat itself indefinitely and thus tend to discount the party as a serious contender for power. Nearly everywhere, noncommunists continue to minimize the Communist threat because of the party's numerical insignificance and to maintain that adequate measures for containing them can be taken if the Communists should become a pressing problem. At the same time, paradoxically, there is growing acceptance of two constantly reiterated propaganda themes which hold, on the one hand, that communism represents the inevitable wave of the future and, on the other, that in Latin America communism in power would evolve along new and special lines compatible with the cultural inheritance of the Latin American people. The history of the Communist movement demonstrates clearly that none of these views is valid and that, indeed, those who hold to them may unwittingly help to convert Communist objectives into reality.

Despite the advantages they seem to enjoy, the Communists are by no means predestined to assume power in Latin America in the foreseeable future. They appreciate better than most non-communists that their hopes for seizing power depend primarily upon the attitudes and actions—or the lack of action—by the governments of the area. They know that they must have considerable freedom of operation in order to propagandize, to campaign, to obstruct, and even to make revolution. They are aware that they must enhance their stature within the nation in order to come to power either by legal means or by violence, for they cannot expect to be imposed on the country by force of foreign arms. The simple fact that Cuba is an island virtually rules out the possibility of its infiltrating a sufficiently large force to topple any Latin American regime, while outright invasion would almost certainly provoke military counteraction by the Organization of American States. The Communists realize that wherever the party is denied legal status and the cooperation of other political groups, and wherever its propaganda apparatus is dismantled, its following and influence quickly dissipate. Therefore, the Latin American Communists may be expected to continue by all means at their disposal to encourage those who feel that nothing *can* be done and those who feel that nothing *need* be done to curb their activities. And they will obviously seek to strengthen the opinion of those anticommunists who hold that even though communism is a potential threat its exponents cannot be denied the right to expound their views.

The minority of anticommunists in Latin America express strong and divergent views about the causes of communism and the best means of combatting it. It is frequently asserted by fervent right-wing opponents of communism that the only effective way to eliminate the threat is to use force, proscribing Communist political activities, smashing the overt party apparatus, and killing, jailing, or exiling its leaders. The noncommunist leftists retaliate that Communists who suffer such oppression take on the mantle of martyrs or popular heroes and that subsequently the party emerges stronger than ever when the oppressive regime finally falls. They usually point out also that governments which adopt repressive anticommunist measures are prone to be indiscriminate in applying the Communist label to all enemies, thereby casting doubt as to the authenticity of its charges against legitimate Communists and further enhancing the respectability of the party when the inevitable day of retribution arrives. There is a strong element of truth in both views, but a review of the history of the Communist movement in Latin America indicates that neither is universally valid.

In the case of the Dominican Republic this conclusion is clearly illustrated. Certainly, during most of the long Trujillo tyranny—and at a terrible price in terms of the personal, civil, and political liberties of the entire population—the Communist movement was so effectively suppressed that to all intents and purposes it ceased to exist in the republic. A handful of exiles maintained the façade of a party wherever they could find temporary haven in neighboring countries and pathetically presumed to speak for the Dominican people at international Communist gatherings. Almost immediately after the dictator was assassinated the Communists began to return to their homeland. According to the noncommunist leftists they should have received a prodigal's welcome, for Trujillo had oppressed them as he had all of his enemies, and he had been less than scrupulous in applying the Communist epithet to noncommunist opponents. The Dominican Communists, however, were rejected by the parties and the populace, and have been obliged to disguise their ideological leanings in order to compete at all with noncommunists for a political following.

The examples of both Haiti and the Dominican Republic demonstrate that communism can be effectively eliminated as long as the government is able and willing to employ full legal measures, police action, and terror against it. But it is too much to expect that a regime capable of resorting to such tactics will confine them exclusively to the Communist opposition. In both countries suppression of the Communist party was incidental to the suppression of all opposition and was accomplished at an inordinate cost to the personal safety and civil liberties of the population at large.

The assertion is commonly heard that communism thrives on poverty and squalor and that where the people have abysmal living standards, where malnutrition, disease, illiteracy, and want are widespread, there communism will flourish. In many parts of Latin America and elsewhere in the world Communists are exploiting precisely such conditions. But nowhere in Latin America and in few places around the globe is the general populace so debased in terms of ignorance, apathy, and material needs as in Haiti, where communism has never exerted an effective appeal. The Haitian example suggests that either the expectations of the public or the caliber of Communist leadership, and probably both, must increase sharply before the lure of communism will find a receptive audience among the people of the republic. In any event, the experience of several Latin American nations in recent decades has shown that the appeal of communism rises as the expectations of the people are raised and frustrated and that improvements in living standards alone are no guarantee against an aggressive and expanding Communist party.

These examples have been cited to point up the fact that there is probably no single remedy for the Communist problem that might be applied throughout Latin America. Clearly, in Cuba the Communists will be removed from power only by violence, but there are means at the disposal of the other republics to deal with the Communist question within the limits of Latin America's political heritage. The past experience of the Latin American Communist parties reveals four sets of circumstances in which Communist prospects are minimal.

1. The appeal of communism does not elicit a favorable response where the party lacks the respectability of legal status and the right, *de facto* or *de jure,* to compete or cooperate as peers with the noncommunist parties.
2. Even though the party enjoys full legal standing, its appeal is not effective where the existing regime is able to satisfy the most pressing demands of the bulk of the population. In Latin America this situation is best illustrated in the case of Mexico.
3. The communist appeal is ineffectual where the party and its front organizations are rigidly suppressed, although the party is apt to revive when the curbs upon its actions are relaxed.
4. Communism works under a serious handicap where those seek-

ing revolutionary change—the restoration of political free-
doms or the elimination of socioeconomic inequities—have an
attractive alternative among opposition political forces. This
alternative does not necessarily have to be a leftist radical
group, but it must promise and seem able to achieve the kinds
of material and psychological reforms for which the underprivileged are clamoring, that is, an improved economic position and an enhanced sense of dignity for the individual.

Except in Cuba the noncommunist parties have been able
to retain the support and sustain the expectations of the great
mass of the Latin American electorate. It seems likely that they
will continue to receive such support only so long as they can
convince a restive and impatient public that its demands for a
better way of life will be fulfilled. Wherever they are able, the
Communists will seek to prevent the fulfillment of this goal,
hoping to ride to power on the wave of frustration and resent-
ment that would certainly follow.

Appendices

Appendix I

MAJOR COMMUNIST PARTIES OF LATIN AMERICA, 1918–1963

Country	Name of Communist or Front Party	Existence as Major Communist or Front Party	Communist Party or Movement Proscribed	Legal Status
Argentina	Communist Party of Argentina (*Partido Comunista de la Argentina*)	1918–	1930–1945, 1959	Illegal
Bolivia	Party of the Revolutionary Left (*Partido de la Izquierda Revolucionaria*)	1940–1949	1940–1943, 1946–1952	
	Communist Party of Bolivia (*Partido Comunista de Bolivia*)	1949–	1946–1952	Legal
Brazil	Communist Party of Brazil (*Partido Comunista do Brasil*)	1922–1961	1922–1945, 1947	
	Brazilian Communist Party (*Partido Comunista Brasileiro*)	1961–		Illegal
Chile	Communist Party of Chile (*Partido Comunista de Chile*)	1921–	1922–1936, 1948–1958	Legal
Colombia	Socialist Revolutionary Party (*Partido Socialista Revolucionario*)	1928–1930		
	Communist Party of Colombia (*Partido Comunista de Colombia*)	1930–1944		
	Social Democratic Party (*Partido Social Democrático*)	1944–1947		

Country		Existence as Major Communist or Front Party	Communist Party or Movement Proscribed	Legal Status
Colombia	Communist Party of Colombia (*Partido Comunista de Colombia*)	1947–	1956–1957	Legal
Costa Rica	Communist Party of Costa Rica (*Partido Comunista de Costa Rica*)	1929–1944		
	Popular Vanguard Party (*Partido Vanguardia Popular*)	1944–	1948	Illegal
Cuba	Communist Party of Cuba (*Partido Comunista de Cuba*)	1925–1939	1925–1938	
	Communist Revolutionary Union (*Unión Revolucionaria Comunista*)	1939–1944		
	Popular Socialist Party (*Partido Socialista Popular*)	1944–1961	1953–1958	
	Integrated Revolutionary Organizations (*Organizaciones Revolucionarias Integradas*)	1961–1963		
	United Party of the Socialist Revolution (*Partido Unido de la Revolución Socialista*)	1963–		Legal
Dominican Republic	Dominican Communist Party (*Partido Comunista Dominicana*)	1942–1946	1942–1946	

225

Country	Name of Communist or Front Party	Existence as Major Communist or Front Party	Communist Party or Movement Proscribed	Legal Status
Dominican Rep. (cont'd.)	Popular Socialist Party (*Partido Socialista Popular*)	1946–	1947	Illegal
Ecuador	Ecuadoran Socialist Party (*Partido Socialista Ecuatoriana*)	1926–1931		
	Communist Party of Ecuador (*Partido Comunista del Ecuador*)	1931–	1931–1944, 1963	Illegal
El Salvador	Communist Party of El Salvador (*Partido Comunista de El Salvador*)	1925–1932, 1944–	1920's, 1952	Illegal
Guatemala	Socialist Labor Unification (*Unificación Obrera Socialista*)	c. 1923–1924		
	Communist Party of Guatemala (*Partido Comunista de Guatemala*)	1925–1932, 1949–1952	1920's–1944	
	Guatemalan Labor Party (*Partido Guatemalteco del Trabajo*)	1952–	1954	Illegal
Haiti	Communist Party of Haiti (*Parti Communiste d'Haiti*)	1930, 1946–1947	1930–1946, 1948	
	Popular Socialist Party (*Parti Socialiste Populaire*)	1946–1949	1949	
	Party of Popular Accord (*Parti d'Entente Populaire*)	1959–		Illegal

226

Country	Name of Communist or Front Party	Existence as Major Communist or Front Party	Communist Party or Movement Proscribed	Legal Status
	People's National Liberation Party (*Parti Populaire de Liberation Nationale*)	1961–		Illegal
Honduras	Communist Party of Honduras (*Partido Comunista de Honduras*)	c. 1928–1932	1920's, 1946	
	Democratic Revolutionary Party of Honduras (*Partido Democrático Revolucionario de Honduras*)	1948–1953		
	Communist Party of Honduras (*Partido Comunista de Honduras*)	1958–		Illegal
Mexico	Mexican Communist Party (*Partido Comunista Mexicano*)	1919–	1929–1935	Legal
	People's Party (*Partido Popular*)	1947–1960		
	Socialist People's Party (*Partido Popular Socialista*)	1960–		Legal
Nicaragua	Workers' Party of Nicaragua (*Partido Obrero de Nicaragua*)	c. 1934–1937		
	Socialist Party of Nicaragua (*Partido Socialista de Nicaragua*)	1937–	1930's, 1945	Illegal

Country	Name of Communist or Front Party	Existence as Major Communist or Front Party	Communist Party or Movement Proscribed	Legal Status
Panama	*Laborista Party* (*Partido Laborista*)	c. 1926–1930		
	Communist Party of Panama (*Partido Comunista del Panamá*)	1930–1944		
	Party of the People (*Partido del Pueblo*)	1944–	1953	Illegal
Paraguay	Paraguayan Communist Party (*Partido Comunista Paraguayo*)	1928–	1936	Illegal
Peru	Peruvian Socialist Party (*Partido Socialista Peruano*)	1928–1930		
	Peruvian Communist Party (*Partido Comunista Peruano*)	1930–	1930's–1945, 1948	Illegal
Uruguay	Communist Party of Uruguay (*Partido Comunista del Uruguay*)	1921–	Never proscribed	Legal
Venezuela	Communist Party of Venezuela (*Partido Comunista de Venezuela*)	1931–	1920's–1945, 1950–1958, 1963	Illegal
	Venezuelan Organization Movement (*Movimiento de Organización Venezolana*)	1936		

Country	Name of Communist or Front Party	Existence as Major Communist or Front Party	Communist Party or Movement Proscribed	Legal Status
	National Democratic Party (*Partido Democrático Nacional*)	1936–1938		
	Venezuelan Popular Union (*Unión Popular Venezolana*)	1943–1946		
	Revolutionary Party of the Communist Proletariat (*Partido Revolucionario del Proletariado* [*comunista*])	1947–1952		

Appendix II

ESTIMATED MEMBERSHIP OF LATIN AMERICAN
COMMUNIST PARTIES IN SELECTED
POSTWAR YEARS

Country	1947	1952	1957	1963
Argentina	30,000	30,000	90,000	50,000
Bolivia	negligible	2,000	5,000	4,000
Brazil	150,000	60,000	50,000	35,000
Chile	50,000	35,000	25,000	30,000
Colombia	5,000	3,000	5,000	8,000
Costa Rica	3,000	2,000	300	300
Cuba	50,000	25,000	12,000	80,000
Dominican Republic	500	negligible	negligible	negligible
Ecuador	2,500	2,000	1,000	3,000
El Salvador	negligible	500	500	500
Guatemala	negligible	1,000	1,000	1,000
Haiti	500	negligible	negligible	negligible
Honduras	negligible	negligible	500	2,000
Mexico	10,000	5,000	5,000	5,000
Nicaragua	500	500	200	300
Panama	500	500	negligible	150
Paraguay	8,000	1,000	500	500
Peru	30,000	10,000	6,000	7,000
Uruguay	15,000	10,000	3,000	4,000
Venezuela	20,000	10,000	9,000	30,000
	375,500	197,500	214,000	260,750

COMMENTS ON SOURCES

The present study is largely the product of research conducted by the author over several years in the Department of State. It is heavily based throughout on materials gleaned from Latin American Communist newspapers and theoretical journals, diplomatic and consular despatches from all areas of Latin America for the years since 1917, and pertinent published reports by the Department of State, the United States Information Agency, and the United States Congress. The study also draws upon the following major international Communist journals: the Comintern's *International Press Correspondence*, for the period prior to the second world war; the Cominform's *For a Lasting Peace, For a People's Democracy!*, for the years 1947 through 1956; and *World Marxist Review: Problems of Peace and Socialism*, for the years since 1958. These sources and the published statutes, programs, and proceedings of National Congresses of the individual Communist parties have provided most of the data included on Communist propaganda, organization, strategy, and objectives in Latin America.

Secondary works on the history of communism in Latin America and on the position of the parties in the international Communist movement are sparse and of widely varying quality. Easily the most authoritative and complete monograph covering the entire region is Robert J. Alexander's *Communism in Latin America*. First published in 1957 and considered a pioneer work in the field, this is a treatise with particular emphasis on communism in the labor movement. An earlier study which sketches much of the history of the Latin American Communist parties and focuses sharply on their relations with the Comintern is Victor Alba's *Historia del comunismo en América Latina.* Both Alexander and Alba have also contributed articles on various facets of the Communist past in the Western Hemisphere in such periodicals as *Problems of Communism,* a valuable source for the specialist and the lay reader alike.

The relations of the Soviet bloc and Communist China with Latin America are capably described and analyzed from the viewpoint of the United States in several studies prepared by independent scholars and by official agencies. The finest brief survey of Soviet political, economic, and cultural relations is *International Communism and Latin America: Perspectives and Prospects,* by Dorothy Dillon, published by the School of Inter-American Studies at the University of Florida. A generally accurate and complete account of Soviet-bloc activities in Latin America before the rise of Castro is found in "Soviet-Bloc Latin American Activities and Their Implications for United States Foreign Policy," issued by the United States Senate in *United States-Latin American Relations.* Two detailed and still useful accounts of the Soviet economic drive in Latin America are the U.S. Department of State's *The Sino-Soviet Economic Offensive in the Less Developed Countries* and Robert Loring Allen's *Soviet Influence in Latin America: The Role of Economic Relations.*

With the exception of the smattering of studies on the Guatemalan Communist adventure in the early 1950's and the post-1959 flood of books and pamphlets on Cuba, there is little available literature in English on the history of individual Latin American Communist parties. In recent years occasional old Communist leaders have published partial accounts of their activities in the early days of the movement, but these and the few official histories and accounts by anticommunists in Latin America should be used with caution. Frequently they are more valuable for what is omitted than for what they include. For the most part the reader must rely on the works of a few foreign scholars for reasonably objective interpretations and commentaries on the Communist parties in the separate republics.

No attempt is made here to include or evaluate the mass of contemporary literature on the Cuban revolution. The authoritative Communist version as of 1960 is found in Blas Roca's *The Cuban Revolution,* while Theodore Draper's *Castro's Revolution: Myths and Realities* probably remains the most searching and objective analysis of the Communist rise to power in Cuba. Irving Pflaum's reports issued by the American Universities Field Staff in 1960 provide keen insights into the effects of the revolution on the Cuban people. A unique current series of reports on the impact of the Castro revolution on the Latin American Communist parties and on their relations with the Soviet Union is that prepared for the Center of International Studies at the Massachusetts Institute of Technology by Ernst Halperin, who examines these questions in the light of long familiarity with communism in Europe.

Ronald Schneider's *Communism in Guatemala, 1944–1954* examines in elaborate detail the techniques employed by the Communists in their nearly successful quest for power in the Central American republic. A well-documented source of information on the early phase of the Communist movement in Guatemala and on the Communist revolt in El Salvador in 1932 is Jorge Schlesinger's *Revolución comunista.*

The completely sympathetic biography of Luiz Carlos Prestes by Jorge Amado, *O cavalheiro da esperança: Vida de Luiz Carlos Prestes,* which has also been published in French and Spanish translations, is an indispensable but not entirely reliable source on the life of Brazil's outstanding Communist.

The Communist experiment with the popular-front technique in Chile is related in John R. Stevenson's *The Chilean Popular Front* and is the principal theme of *The Yenan Way,* by Peruvian ex-Communist Eudocio Ravines. Ravines' account, moreover, contains excellent material on the origins of the Communist movement in Peru and on the activities of various Latin American Communists in the Comintern.

The forthcoming history of communism in Mexico by Karl M. Schmitt will fill the need for a thorough examination of the first four decades of the Communist movement in that country.

Interesting details on the origins of the Mexican Communist party may be found in Carleton Beals's *Glass Houses: Ten Years of Free Lancing* and in Bertram D. Wolfe's excellent biography *Diego Rivera*. The author is indebted to Dr. Wolfe for many details and comments on the early years of the Communist party in Mexico.

The following selected bibliography includes the works listed above and other leading studies—in English, Spanish, and Portuguese—which deal with one or more aspects of communism in Latin America.

SELECTED BIBLIOGRAPHY

Alexander, Robert J. *Communism in Latin America.* New Brunswick, N.J.: Rutgers University Press, 1957.

Alba, Victor. *Historia del comunismo en América Latina.* México, D.F., México: Ediciones Occidentales, 1954.

Allen, Robert Loring. *Soviet Influence in Latin America: The Role of Economic Relations.* Washington, D.C.: Public Affairs Press, 1959.

Amado, Jorge. *O cavalheiro da esperança: Vida de Luiz Carlos Prestes.* Tenth edition. Rio de Janeiro, Brazil: Editorial Vitória, 1956.

——— *O mundo da paz.* Rio de Janeiro, Brazil: Editorial Vitória, 1951.

Beals, Carleton. *Glass Houses: Ten Years of Free Lancing.* New York: J. B. Lippincott Company, 1938.

Crespo Toral, Jorge. *El comunismo en el Ecuador.* Quito, Ecuador, 1958.

Dillon, Dorothy. *International Communism and Latin America: Perspectives and Prospects.* Latin American Monograph, No. 19, School of Inter-American Studies, University of Florida. Gainesville, Fla.: University of Florida Press, 1962.

Draper, Theodore. *Castro's Revolution: Myths and Realities.* New York: Frederick A. Praeger, Inc., 1962.

For a Lasting Peace, For a People's Democracy!, Vols. I-X. Published in Bucharest and simultaneously in other cities, 1947–1956.

Halperin, Ernst. *Castro and Latin American Communism.* Cambridge, Mass., 1963. This is one of a continuing series of reports prepared for and published by the International Communism Project, Center for International Studies, Massachusetts Institute of Technology.

International Press Correspondence. Vols. I-XVIII. Vienna, Berlin, London, 1921–1938.

James, Daniel. *Red Design for the Americas: Guatemalan Prelude.* New York: The John Day Co., 1954.

Kirkpatrick, Evron M. (ed.). *Target the World.* New York: The Macmillan Company, 1956.

Lafertte, Elías. *Vida de un comunista: Páginas autobiográficas.* Santiago, Chile: Talleres Gráficos Horizonte, 1961.

Partido Comunista de la Argentina. *Esbozo de historia del partido comunista de la Argentina.* Buenos Aires, Argentina: Editorial Anteo, 1947.

Partido Comunista de Chile. *Ricardo Fonseca, combatiente ejemplar.* Santiago, Chile, 1952 (?).

Partido Comunista do Brasil. "O IV Congresso do partido comunista do Brasil," *Problemas, Revista mensal de cultura política,* No. 64 (Dec., 1954–Feb., 1955), 1–414.

Partido Socialista Popular. *VIII asamblea nacional: Informes, resoluciones, programa, estatutos.* Habana, Cuba: Ediciones Populares, 1960.

Pereira, Astrojildo. *Formação do PCB, 1922/1928.* Rio de Janeiro, Brasil: Editorial Vitória, 1962.

Pflaum, Irving P. "Castro's Cuba in Mid-1960: Some Over-all Impressions of the Revolution," *American Universities Field Staff Reports Service,* Mexico and Caribbean Area Series, Vol. V, No. 1 (Cuba, August 1960), 1–22. This is the first in a series of six reports.

Ramos, Jorge Abelardo. *El partido comunista en la política argentina. Su historia y su crítica.* Buenos Aires, Argentina: Coyoacán, 1962.

Ravines, Eudocio. *The Yenan Way.* New York: Charles Scribner's Sons, 1951.

Roca, Blas [Francisco Calderío]. *The Cuban Revolution.* New York: New Century Publishers, 1961.

Schlesinger, Jorge. *Revolución comunista*. Guatemala: Editorial Unión, 1946.

Schneider, Ronald M. *Communism in Guatemala, 1944–1954*. New York: Frederick A. Praeger, Inc., 1958.

Stevenson, John Reese. *The Chilean Popular Front*. Philadelphia: University of Pennsylvania Press, 1942.

U.S. Department of State. *The Sino-Soviet Economic Offensive in the Less Developed Countries*. Publication 6632. Washington, D.C.: U.S. Government Printing Office, May, 1958.

────── *World Strength of the Communist Party Organizations*. IR Nos. R-8 to R-15. Washington, D.C.: U.S. Government Printing Office, 1956–1963.

U.S. Information Agency. *Problems of Communism*. Vols. I-XII. Washington, D.C.: U.S. Government Printing Office, 1952–1963.

U.S. Senate. "Soviet Bloc Latin American Activities and Their Implications for United States Foreign Policy,"*United States-Latin American Relations*. Washington, D.C.: U.S. Government Printing Office, February, 1960.

Wolfe, Bertram D. *Diego Rivera*. New York: Alfred A. Knopf, Inc., 1939.

World Marxist Review: Problems of Peace and Socialism. This journal has appeared monthly since 1958. English language editions are published in Great Britain and Canada.

Index

Aguirre Cerda, Pedro, 145–146
Albania, 162, 197, 198
Alessandri, Arturo, 67–69
Alexis, Jacques Stephen, 17
Alfaro Siqueiros, David, 44, 64–65, 100, 111–112, 124
Alliance of Democratic Youth of Guatemala, 133
Alliance for Progress, 5, 51–52
Amado, Jorge, 44, 167
Anti-Imperialist League, 156
APRA (American Popular Revolutionary Alliance), 15, 83
Aprista parties, 24n, 40–41
Arbenz, Jacobo, 36, 93, 196
Argentina, 11–12, 20, 31, 32, 36, 57, 58–61, 63n, 79, 108, 113, 131, 159, 160, 192, 195, 197, 199, 200
Arismendi, Rodney, 112
Armed forces, 107–108
Arroyo del Río, Carlos, 147n
Assemblies, 125
Association of Latin American Labor Unions, 131

Baliño, Carlos, 80
Baron, Victor Allan, 144
Barthe, Obdulio, 82, 111
Base organizations, 125
Batista, Fulgencio, 81–82, 102, 115, 141 173, 179–180, 181, 187, 196
Becerra, Gustavo, 85
Belaunde, Fernando, 15
Berger, Harry. See Arthur Ernst Ewert

Bernardes, Artur, 73
Betancourt, Rómulo, 8, 86
Binational centers, 136–137, 176
Bolivia, 10–11, 24n, 79, 89, 94, 147, 157, 194, 196, 197
Bolivian-Czechoslovakian Friendship Center, 136
Borodin, Michael, 62, 152, 154
Bosch, Juan, 9
Brandão, Octavio, 71, 75, 161
Brazil, 5, 12–15, 26, 31, 56–57, 58, 70–78, 79, 108, 135, 136, 143–144, 147, 155, 158, 159, 160, 161, 166, 167, 192, 194, 195, 196, 197, 198, 199, 200, 201–202, 210
Brazilian Communist Party, 14
Brazilian Cooperative Syndicalist Confederation, 73
Brazil-Poland Center of Studies and University Exchange, 136
Bulgaria, 136, 162, 197, 198, 199

Calderío, Francisco. See Blas Roca
Campa, Valentín, 113
Canelas, Antonio, 72
Carías, Tiburcio, 84, 94
Carranza, Venustiano, 61
Carrillo Puerto, Felipe, 63–64
Castillo Armas, Carlos, 94
Castro, Fidel, 7, 45, 95, 102, 107, 115, 140, 166, 170, 173, 177, 178ff., 192, 200, 202, 203, 205, 217
Cells, 119, 125–126
Central committee, 119, 120, 121–122, 123, 126